The Wise Woman Builds

How To Build A Godly Home In An Ungodly World

By

Golden Keyes Parsons

"The wise woman builds her house, but with her own hands the foolish one tears hers down" (Proverbs 14:1).

PRESS

DEDICATION

To all the Wise Women in my life who have loved, supported and been a part of this conference/Bible study--especially my critique group, Linda Jewell, Marita Littauer, Sherrie Buerkle and Raelene Searle . To my mom, Lois Clark Keyes, who passed away this year, but who believed I was a Wise Woman. To our three daughters, Amber, Andra and Amanda, who have matured into Wise Women. To my husband, Blaine, who encouraged me in my journey to become a Wise Woman.

And to my Lord Jesus, who is Wisdom.

Table of Contents

Introduction

"I'm not in love with my husband anymore." The beautiful young woman sat in our office with dry eyes and a shattered marriage. She stared defiantly at us as she nervously fidgeted with her large expensive silver earrings. Her long, thick black hair framed her angular tanned face. Sparks of tension filled the air.

"Don't I need to be in love with my husband in order for the marriage to work? We have drifted apart. He's always working. He has a mistress. It is his job, and he will always choose his mistress above me. He leaves me alone all the time and pays me no attention. We never go out for dinner or to a movie. I am lonely. The love is gone."

They had no children and her husband was obsessed with his job. They lived in a lovely home, wore nice clothes and drove new cars. What had happened to this articulate, well-educated, attractive couple? This woman felt she needed to be passionately, romantically in love with her husband at all times, through all circumstances, or the marriage could not be saved. She could not trust that God would restore the love. Had the worldly "Hollywood" philosophy of constant hot-white lust and romance blinded her? She left him, and they divorced. The house crumbled.

* * * * * *

An attractive, slightly overweight young woman with a loving husband and three children quickly started her car and motioned for me to get in the passenger side. "I don't want to come to the end of my life and have regrets because I didn't reach my full potential."

Her mother was lying in a hospital bed dying of cancer, and this young woman was burning the candle at both ends to meet all her obligations. As a result, her family was teetering on the brink of disaster. She and her husband were a part of our young couple's small group. We baby-sat each other's children. Our husbands were accountability partners.

Cars whizzed along the interstate in the background as we drove through the late evening traffic. Her dark eyes, which normally twinkled brightly above her wide smile, darted back and forth nervously between the rear view mirror, the oncoming traffic and my gaze of surprise.

"Your mother is dying, your marriage is falling apart, and you are worried about your potential?" I cried out in astonishment. "Get your priorities in order!" My youthful "counsel" was not very tactful, nor helpful. In the ensuing years, I wished I had exhibited more compassion and caring.

She did, indeed, have a very promising career in fashion marketing. She was in upper management of the leading modeling agency in a city known as one of the fashion centers of the country. Her star was rising. She was highly respected in her field in this metropolitan area.

Her mother passed away a few weeks later. Her family eventually fell apart, and they divorced, as she went on to fulfill the need she had to be a successful career woman. Could it be the priorities in this relationship were based on the "wisdom" of the world, rather than on God's wisdom?

* * * * * *

I sat beside my childhood best friend, as she wept bitter, anguished tears over her husband's affair. We were together constantly in our early years—spending the night together, going

swimming, learning to dance, meeting at the movies. We shared the agony and ecstasy of

boyfriends during high school, staying up late in the night giggling and plotting our strategy for

the next time we would see the current heart throb. She was my main encourager when I ran for

cheerleader at our high school and nobody else dreamed the poor little girl from the other side of

the tracks could possibly win the elections. My tears flowed with hers as I realized now that

when she needed encouraging, I could not help her. Her shoulders shook as the sobbing came

and went. She fought to gain composure.

"I've done everything I know to do to keep the marriage together and now this. I simply

don't know what else to do."

They had been married almost thirty years. Her husband made the choice to enter an

adulterous affair, and it destroyed their marriage. Had the "feel good" attitude of our secular

society been the downfall of this marriage?

* * * * * *

Why were these houses crumbling now? What had been left undone as these Christian

couples built their homes? What does it mean for a wise woman to build her house? Each one of

these unions professed to be a Christian marriage. Each marriage had committed to make Jesus

Christ the head of their home. This study will take a look at what godly wisdom is, what it means

to be a wise woman who builds her house, how a woman foolishly tears down her house with her

own hands, and what to do to prevent the downfall of one's family.

Throughout the study you will find questions and places to fill in your answers. This

project can be undertaken individually or in a small group setting, however, it is my feeling that it will be most effective going through the material with a group. But if you do not have a gathering of Christian sisters with which to meet, dive in by yourself. Or perhaps you could find just one other girlfriend with whom to go through the study.

Scattered throughout you will find a *"Building Tool"* heading which is an indication of a practical assignment for you to do: a Scripture to memorize and quote to a friend, a topic to discuss with your spouse, a prayer to write out. Just as a builder picks up a hammer or saw or drill and begins to bring the blueprints of a house to reality, the *"Building Tools"* will bring the theory of the Bible study to life. Don't skip these assignments. At the end are blank pages to write down your personal perceptions as you go through the study.

All the Scriptures quoted are from the NIV version, unless otherwise indicated. Sometimes I ask you to read a Scripture from different versions. Just gather together three or four versions to have handy as you begin to study: King James, New King James, New American Standard, The Living Bible, The Amplified Bible, The Message. Any of those are fine.

Whenever I have given the meanings of Hebrew or Greek words, I have used Strong's Concordance. If you do not have one, you can get Bible software that contains it, or you can purchase a small, paperback version at your local Christian bookstore to aid you in your study if you like.

My heart is emblazoned on this study. My passion is that homes, which claim Jesus Christ as their Lord and Master, be abundantly full of love and joy and wisdom. Please know that much prayer, years of lessons learned the hard way and of pastoring have gone into this book. I am praying for you as you seek God's face to become "The Wise Woman Who Builds."

Chapter One

The Wise Woman

What Is A Wise Woman?

One of the few verses in Proverbs addressed directly to women is the theme verse for this study, Proverbs 14:1:

The wise woman builds her house, but with her own hands the foolish one tears hers down.

From that observation, we can assume that it must be important for us as women to heed the admonition.

- Read Proverbs 14:1 in several different translations and note that the verse is very similar in almost every version. What kind of woman builds her house?

- What kind of woman tears down her own house?

- Would you say, then, that the opposite of a wise person is a foolish person?

How do we learn to be wise rather than foolish? The Scripture is full of principles and counsel to show us the path to wisdom. Let's begin by looking at a familiar Psalm.

- Read Psalm 1:1-2 and, in your own words, list what a wise person does not do and what a wise person does.

<u>What a wise person does not do</u>   <u>What a wise person does</u>

- What does Psalm 1:3 tell us are the results of acting wisely?

- Take those results we gleaned from Psalm 1:3 and apply them to the marriage relationship. What might they be?

Before we continue, perhaps we should take a look at the word "wisdom." Later we will be talking about worldly wisdom vs. godly wisdom, so let's get a handle on what we mean. In the secular sphere, wisdom might be viewed as the expertise of knowing how to live successfully, or a philosophy of life. In the Christian sense, a precise definition of the word "wisdom" is not simple, due, in part, to the poetic language found in the wisdom literature of Job, Psalms, Proverbs, the Song of Solomon, Ecclesiastes and Lamentations.

For the purposes of this study, we will adopt the definition of "wisdom" as found in the Amplified Bible's translation of Proverbs 4:11:

I have taught you in the way of skillful and godly Wisdom (which is comprehensive insight into the ways and purposes of God); I have led you in paths of uprightness.

"Comprehensive insight into the ways and purposes of God"—seeing the circumstances of life with God's perspective. This will serve as our operative definition of "wisdom" and is the goal of this study.

What is a foolish woman?

- What are the characteristics of a wicked or foolish person as seen in Psalm 1:4-5?

In the Wisdom Literature of Psalms and Proverbs, the word "fool" does not mean a moron or an imbecile, but it means one who is rebellious and does not fear the Lord.

- Therefore, when Proverbs 14:1 says the foolish woman tears down her house with her own hands, what, in your own words, is the writer of Proverbs telling us?

- What do you think "with her own hands," means?

Worldly "Wisdom"

In the September 8, 2004, *Barna Update*, George Barna reports that overall, 35% of all born again individuals who have been married have gone through a divorce, identical to the 35% incidence among non-born-again adults. "A person's faith doesn't seem to have a lot of effect on whether they'll get divorced," Barna says. "Even among born-again Christians, most don't exhibit attitudes or behaviors any different than non-Christians."

These are alarming statistics and should concern believers. What are we to do with this as Christian women? Are Christian young women adequately prepared to build their houses as they embark upon the tumultuous sea of matrimony? It doesn't appear they are according to the quoted figures.

- Compare the following categories, which our culture considers valid reasons for divorce with what Scripture teaches. Write the Scriptural solution below each problem.

<u>What our culture says:</u>   <u>What Scripture says:</u>

1. Incompatibility   I Peter 3:1

2. Lack of love   Titus 2:4-5; Ephesians 5:25

3. Irreconcilable differences   Ephesians 5:21

4. No Fault   Ephesians 5:25-27

5. Adultery   The Book of Hosea; Matt 19:1-9

- Is there any reason given above that Scripture says is a valid reason for divorce? Which one?

- Does that mean a marriage can never be saved if the above takes place?

- In Matthew 19:1-9, we find what Jesus told his disciples about God's perspective on divorce. Write down below your understanding of what He said.

Certainly, there are occasions when valid reasons for divorce are present. Abuse and unfaithfulness present tough situations that call for great wisdom in addressing. Especially in abusive instances, separation is recommended, and many times is essential. And there are other difficult, complicated circumstances: mental illness, abandonment, medical trauma (such as a mate in a coma for years), and missing persons. I recall a couple who came to our retreat center for a couple's conference. They were a very handsome pair, but the husband had suffered a severe head injury in a car accident. He was badly impaired. He walked with a limp and could not use one of his arms. His speech was strained and garbled. But his beautiful wife stayed literally by his side assisting him to perform the simplest of tasks. She remained by his side, as his wife, fulfilling her conviction that she live out her commitment to him, for better, for worse, in sickness and in health. The answers aren't always easy and sometimes, however, divorce regrettably occurs in complex cases such as this.

When our hearts are breaking, and we feel we are total failures, we fall on the mercy of a compassionate God who loves us and will work out the plans for our lives, in spite of our failures or those of our mates.

- ***Building Tool*** - Read Psalm 145 and meditate on it. Write out below verses 8, 9 and 14 and memorize them. Ask a friend to hold you accountable and quote the verses to her.

- Read Jeremiah 29:11. The Amplified Bible ends the verse this way, "…to give you hope in your final outcome." Even though you may be divorced, according to this verse, is there any reason for despair?

  Why or why not?

The reasons for divorce in today's culture are varied and complicated, and I do not mean to suggest pious platitudes as solutions for wrenching situations.

This startling e-mail from a Christian wife came to us recently: "I am writing with very bad news and asking for prayer. My husband left me Sunday for another woman he has been having an affair with for a year. The children and I are in shock and agony."

This couple was in ministry. He was a Christian counselor, an elder in their church and a professor at a seminary. Not only that, but they taught and led marriage conferences for years. They led the marriage conference that was instrumental in restoring our marriage, and we joined them in leading several other conferences. Dealing with so many broken marriages as pastors, we are beyond being shocked at most anything, but I must admit, this one shocked me.

Sometimes no matter how much prayer is offered, no matter how much one "stands by the marriage," no matter who it is, the enemy can secure inroads in the marriage relationship by using his master ploy of deceit. The deceit takes over, and Satan is victorious in destroying the marriage. When one is in the midst of deceit, it is very difficult to see the truth. Obviously this husband had been deceived and stepped over the line. The sticky web of the world's wisdom ensnared him, and the marriage collapsed.

- ***Building Tool*** - Name one way in which you have been deceived and fallen prey to "worldly wisdom" instead of applying Scripture to your marriage.

- Using a Bible Concordance find a Scripture that addresses the problem you listed above and write it out below:

Proverbs 14:12 says, "There is a way that seems right to a man, but in the end it leads to death." Many times the ways of the world *seem* right and logical and appear to prove the Bible outdated or irrelevant or illogical. But time after time the Scripture stands as scientists and psychologists come back around to what is written in the Word.

I am reminded of a very simple example in the field of science. For thousands of years people believed the earth to be flat. But Scripture plainly declares in Isaiah 40:22 that the Lord "...sits enthroned above the *circle* of the earth." (Emphasis mine). It was right there in Scripture for those who would see. Biblical principles will always stand the test of time, whether in the area of science, history or marriage and the family.

- Can you think of another example of how something in Scripture has been considered out-of-date and irrelevant or illogical and then science or history or child psychology proved that the Bible was correct after all?

- Find the Scriptures to support these seemingly illogical or backwards principles according to God's ways:

(1) *Give and it shall be given….*

(2) *Whoever loses his life for my sake shall find it….*

(3) *The Son of Man came not to be ministered unto, but to minister.*

(4) *The first shall be last.*

Many times God's wisdom seems diametrically opposed to logical thinking. A wise woman needs wisdom, God's wisdom, to be a godly wife and raise her children to be a godly heritage in these precarious days. Sometimes the job will seem overwhelming, but the Architect of our lives is at the drafting table drawing up a perfect blueprint for your life. Sometimes the storms will come, but the foundation of Jesus Christ is sure. Sometimes you will feel you don't have the right tools, but they are close at hand in the Word of God. I pray that going through this study will enable you to celebrate the faithfulness of God as you see Him undergirding your efforts to build your homes as a wise woman.

- **Building Tool** - Write out a prayer below confessing times that you have depended upon worldly wisdom instead of godly wisdom. (Be specific.) Express your desire to

be a wise woman who builds her house according to godly wisdom and not the

philosophy of the world.

Small Group Discussion: Share what you have learned about worldly wisdom

versus godly wisdom in today's lesson.

Chapter Two

Count the Cost

"I never was in love with my husband, but his ex-wife had left him with a precious infant son. I was unable to have children, and I fell in love with the baby."

* * * * * *

"We thought because we were in love, everything would work out."

* * * * * *

"I married my husband because I thought we would have a lot of money and live well, but my husband did not pursue the professional career he had started. We don't have the lifestyle I thought we would. I'm just not happy."

* * * * * *

Week after week, month after month, my husband and I watch a parade of couples come through our office and hear the reasons why marriages falter. "Reasons" that illustrate a lack of

forethought concerning the commitment and work involved in making a marriage successful.

- Read Luke 14:28. What is Jesus telling us about marriage in this passage?

Too many times, after the honeymoon is over and the excitement dies down, couples

recognize they don't have all the ingredients necessary to complete the task. They realize that

this phenomenon called marriage is a marathon, not a sprint. They have started on a journey for

which they are not prepared.

- List some ways in which you were ill prepared to build your marriage.

"Marathon Marriage"
(Covenant)

As my husband and I counsel with couples, we inevitably end up talking about

commitment. It all boils down to a relationship in which we have agreed to commit our whole

being. All the other side issues, although some may be deeply painful and serious, really are just

that—side issues. Whether it is love lost, or a wife who doesn't like the lifestyle her husband

provides, or a husband who doesn't understand his wife, or even, in some cases, unfaithfulness, it still boils down to commitment. Is the couple going to honor the commitment, made before God, to stay together until death parts them, despite how arduous it may be to work through the difficulties?

- In Malachi 2:14, we find God's view on marriage. In the context of this passage, God is reproving his people for profaning their marriage vows. What does he call marriage?

- Look up Proverbs 2:17. What does God call marriage in this verse?

- Ezekiel 16:8 says, "…when I saw you and saw that you were old enough for love, I spread the corner of my garment over you" … "spreading the corner of my garment" was a symbolic term for the marriage relationship. Then the Lord says, "I gave you my solemn oath and entered into a covenant with you …" From these verses, how do you perceive God views the marriage vows?

Marriage, in God's eyes, is a covenant alliance, but in western culture, we have little understanding of what that means. Coming to the marriage altar is not making a vow, even though we talk of "taking the marriage vows." Marriage is a covenant, and there is a difference. A vow may involve only one party. For instance, I can vow to lose ten pounds in time for my high school reunion. I can break that vow to myself. Or a vow may involve two or more and can be broken. But a covenant *always* involves two or more and is permanently binding. An oath is taken and the covenant is made, never to be broken. Our culture is a contract culture—contracts being broken on every hand, with little thought to the integrity of one's name on the dotted line.

The Hebrew word for covenant is *berit*. It literally meant "a cutting" and came to mean a contract, a will, a league, a testament, or a bond. In ancient cultures, a cutting of the skin actually took place and blood was exchanged to signify the seriousness of the bond (Gen. 15). Sometimes gifts were exchanged (Gen. 21:30) and/or a pile of stones set up (Gen. 31:53). When a couple stands before a minister and promises to live together in covenant until death parts them, that is a solemn occasion. Covenant is not to be taken lightly.

Lawmakers in some of the United States have noted with alarm the high divorce statistics and have passed legislation invoking covenant marriage laws. Katherine Spaht, LSU Law Center, was instrumental in passing covenant marriage legislation in Louisiana in 1997. Ms. Spaht, speaking at the Christian Marriage, Family and Couples Education (CMFCE) Annual Conference in 1998, had this to say:

> *What the covenant law marriage… represents is an opportunity for virtue, an opportunity to choose a more binding commitment…What covenant marriage does is to ensconce in the law the ideal that marriage is to be a lifelong institution. It doesn't impose, but it permits couples to chose this ideal…Secondly, it was envisioned as a way of revitalizing and reinvigorating what we call mediating structures, human communities, those that nourish and act as coffers between the State and the individual. Principal among those, which covenant marriage encourages and reinvigorates, is the church. It invites religion back into the public square to perform a function it is uniquely situated to do, to preserve marriages.*

> *"Covenant marriage strengthens marriage in three different ways. First, there is mandatory premarital counseling. The second…there is a legally binding agreement that*

if difficulties arise during the marriage, they will take all reasonable steps to preserve the marriage, including marital counseling... It is a form of, in a sense, mandatory pre-divorce counseling. Lastly, ... there are limited grounds for divorce, so it is more difficult to terminate a covenant marriage and more time consuming.

In the passing of covenant marriage laws in some of our states, perhaps even secular society is beginning to recognize that something must be done to help stem the tide of divorces and assist couples in counting the cost.

- Do you think a "wise woman" would be interested in committing to a covenant marriage, rather than a conventional one, if she and her husband lived in a state that provided the opportunity to do so? Why, or why not?

Why Covenant?

In preparing for this study I did much reading on the subject of covenant. Initially I asked the Lord, "Why covenant? Where is the romance? Covenant seems a bit harsh, binding and cold." But as I continued to study, I realized it is the opposite. God created us for covenant relationships. His relationship with us is a covenant relationship. Read the following Scriptures and paraphrase in your own words:

- Isaiah 43:2

- Hebrews 13:5

- Ephesians 5:25

- Revelation 3:20.

God created us for covenant relationships. Covenant is the avenue by which he has related to his people through the ages—Adam, Noah, Abraham, Moses, and the New Covenant, which Jesus *cut* for us with his blood. Covenant provides the safe environment we need in order to grow and reach our full potential—free from all fear of rejection and betrayal. God designed us for permanent relationships. That's why we are shattered over broken relationships, whether by death or divorce, or simply a misunderstanding between two parties in a relationship.

In his teachings on covenant marriage, Jimmy Evans, senior pastor at Trinity Fellowship in Amarillo, TX, says that people engage in basically four types of relationships:

1. Carnal – A business type relationship. You have something I want, and I enter into a relationship with you to get what I want. In business that's acceptable, but not in personal relationships. We see this all the time in our society. Young girls have entered into a relationship with a boy, who simply wants sex, and she has a baby, but no permanent relationship with the baby's father. There is no security in this type of relationship.

2. Consumer – This relationship says, "I'll give to the degree that I benefit." Very similar to the carnal relationship, except there is a cost/benefit ratio here. It is

performance based, such as employer/employee. As long as the employee performs, he is paid what he is worth. It is viable in the work place, but not in a marriage relationship. What happens if one partner becomes ill and can't "perform?" Or when a "better deal" comes along?

3. <u>Conditional</u> – As long as the conditions are good in the marriage, then the partner will stick around. But, if times get hard financially, or again, if illness strikes, what then? "For better or for worse, for richer or poorer, in sickness or in health…" mean very little to most people.

Pastor Evans claims that 90 per cent of the relationships in America are either carnal, consumer or conditional. A constant fear of rejection and betrayal surrounds the marriage relationship and neither partner can give his/her best.

4. <u>Covenant</u> – In this relationship, each partner agrees to die to everything that would break covenant. It means "until death do us part." All fear of rejection is gone, and each partner can completely open up their hearts and be intimate.

In the Jewish culture, even the betrothal or engagement period is secured in covenant. If we try to build a marriage-type relationship outside of covenant, we are very insecure. We build walls of defense around ourselves. Intimacy is difficult, if not impossible.

Satan hates covenant. He will fight to destroy covenant relationships more than almost anything else. He wants to see Christian marriages topple. He hates intimate community among believers. He loves to stir up discord among the brethren. That is because he knows the power of the testimony of covenant relationships to the glory of God.

- *Building Tool* - Have you and your spouse committed to a covenant relationship? Review with your spouse your marriage vows and determine if, whether in actual statements or not, your relationship is a covenant relationship.

- In light of the nature of covenant, do you feel pre-nuptial agreements have a place in a Christian marriage?

  Why or why not?

Leave and Cleave

In the Matthew 19 passage, Jesus addresses divorce and the issue of leaving and cleaving. The two are closely related. To leave means to break away from a dependent relationship in order to form a new relationship. When a husband and wife come together to become one flesh, the old relationship of being under the authority of the parents is left behind. The Hebrew word for leave actually means to abandon, to leave behind, to forsake. The parents move from being in authority over the child to a position of counsel.

A friend of mine and I were discussing the issue of leaving and cleaving. She made the statement that although she was raised in the church and had walked with the Lord a long time, she was not sure she really understood what the terminology "leaving and cleaving" meant.

As we visited, we moved on to another topic involving the family business which she had taken over from her parents several years ago. During the past year my friend had to make some hard decisions in regard to the business with which her parents disagreed. They were very upset.

My friend was grieved over the issue.

"That's what I am talking about," I said to her. "You are no longer under their authority. You are to honor them and listen to their counsel, but when you and your husband married, you left them to cleave to your husband. They no longer have authority over your decisions."

"Cleave" means to "stick like glue" to another. It can only be accomplished after leaving. I heard someone say that most marriage problems are either a matter of leaving improperly or cleaving improperly. When I first heard the remark, I was not sure that generalization could be made across the board. However, in our experience, my husband and I find that it certainly is a major issue. I asked a friend who is a marriage and family therapist if he agreed with the allegation. He thought for a moment and then answered in the affirmative. He agreed that many marital problems sprout from this root topic of leaving and cleaving improperly.

- Name some specific problems in your marriage you have had pertaining to the issue of "leaving and cleaving."

- Have you ever been guilty of emotionally "cleaving" to someone other than your spouse? Explain.

- Would you say this could be an instance of "tearing down your house with your own hands?"

Many times we have sat in our office with couples in whose marriages the emotions have vanished or have been stolen away by another person. We literally beg them to take God at His Word. We plead with them to "cleave," to stick like glue to their mates, and trust Jesus to restore the emotions and redeem the marriage.

The question then becomes, which has the stronger pull in one's life? Is the Word of God more true and strong, or are one's emotions more true and strong? Which choice is going to be made? Which way are the scales tilted—toward God's Word or toward the emotions? When a husband or wife is torn and hurting emotionally, it is difficult to press through. But our God is faithful and will honor our commitment to stand by what Scripture teaches.

- Which has the stronger pull in your life – your emotions or the Word of God?

- If you are divorced, do you feel that it was an irreconcilable situation or do you wish you had been more willing to stay in covenant and "stick like glue"? Explain.

As a wise woman enters into a marriage relationship, she must count the cost. Is she willing to enter into covenant marriage and remain in covenant no matter what difficulties or storms may come? Is she willing to leave and cleave—ready to leave her parents in order to become one with her husband? Willing to stick like glue? As a wise woman is building her home, she must count the cost. If not, she may find herself tearing her house down with her own hands.

Some of the questions in this chapter have been difficult, but Romans 8:1 says,

"Therefore there is now no condemnation for those who are in Christ Jesus." We serve a loving God.

- ***Building Tool*** – Review the Psalm 145:8,9,14 passage you memorized in the first lesson. Write a prayer and thank God for his mercy and compassion and determine to press on.

- ***Small Group Discussion:*** Discuss the concepts of "covenant versus contract" and "leaving and cleaving" with your group. What adjustments, if any, do you need to make in your marriage relationship pertaining to these two areas?

Chapter Three

Who Is Your Architect?

Most of us had an idyllic picture of marriage in our heads as we were growing up—a handsome, understanding, gentle husband; beautiful well-mannered children; a lovely home with a white picket fence. In your mind's eye, picture your dream house. Visualize the layout of the house, the elevation. Is it brick or frame or logs or cedar siding? What color is the carpet? What kind of paneling did you choose? Picture that frilly little girl's room and the luxurious marble sunken tub in the master bathroom.

- Take a moment before we proceed. Go ahead – let's close our eyes and dream. Write a description below.

My husband and I were able to build our dream house at one point in our lives. It was a lovely two-story, Cape Cod style home, on a lush, half-acre wooded lot. I chose old Chicago brick for the exterior, a large colonial fireplace, lots of windows and wood floors. Your dream home may be southwestern adobe style, or Tudor, or perhaps an old country farmhouse you would like to completely refurbish.

Now that we have this beautiful dream house in mind, let's think about something. Did you picture the architect in your mind's eye? Surprisingly, very few of us do. But none of us would argue that the architect is the most valuable starting point of the team in building a house. If the blueprints are not accurate, the house will be a mess. A house can be built without a good architect, but it will be a hodge-podge of disjointed rooms with an awkward flow and a loss of efficiency and warmth.

Recently I noticed an old cabin out in a pasture. It appeared to be an old homestead, long abandoned. The house was leaning so much to one side, that the old roof was almost touching the ground. I wondered how much time would pass before it completely tumbled. The architect of that house must not have used his plumb line correctly. He must not have taken accurate measurements. He may have been hasty in erecting the structure, or did not use good solid materials. Something was faulty in the plans, because now, years later, the house was crumbling.

- Let's look at Jeremiah 29:11. *"For I know the plans I have for you," declares the Lord, "plans to prosper you and not to harm you, plans to give you hope and a future."* Read this verse now in light of a blueprint for your life. Does that put a new perspective on the verse for you?

30

In what way?

The Lord God Almighty is the Architect of our lives, and he has plans for good in mind for us. The plumb line is accurate. He is precise in his measurements. He is not hasty in erecting the structure of our lives, and he uses good, solid materials. Many of us have difficulty believing that God desires good for us. We look at him as some "cosmic killjoy" sitting in heaven looking for a chance to destroy all our dreams and ambitions. But God desires abundant lives for us.

- Read Romans 8:28 from several different translations. Read John 10:10 in the various translations. What do these verses tell you God desires for you?

You may have heard Romans 8:28 glibly thrown at you while you were going through a rough time. "And we know that in all things God works for the good of those who love him, who have been called according to his purpose." Perhaps we even nodded sagely and agreed. But, how many of us believe the truth of Romans 8:28 deep in our spirits and are willing to stake our lives on the goodness of God?

As I have thought about this verse, I believe my favorite part is not the *...in all things God works for good...* phrase, but the *... And we know ...* part. When the pieces of our lives lie at our feet, and we see no way they can be put back together, that verse must come to life for us: *And we know*" – not "Well, I *think* maybe ...." or "I sure *hope* so ... "

- Let's dissect this verse.

  1. In what things do we know God works good?

2. What does God do on our behalf?

3. Is it for our benefit or for our catastrophe?

4. For whom does He work?

5. For what purpose are we called?

- As we can see, it doesn't say *some* things. It says *all* things.

- It doesn't say all things are *good*, it says all things *work together* for good.

- And it doesn't say that all things work together for good for *everybody*. It says that all things work together for good *for those who love Him and are called according to His purpose.*

- Read the next verse—Romans 8:29. To what end is God working in our lives?

- ***Building Tool*** - If you don't already know these verses by memory, write them out below and memorize.

All things work together for good for those who are walking in faith believing the Great Architect to work things out in their behalf according to his purpose, his sovereign blueprint, his plan. When we begin to doubt in the darkness of bad times what we learned in the light of good times, we can trust the goodness of God. We can continue to walk. He is faithful. We can trust him. He is the Great Architect of our lives.

- Turn to Genesis 1 and read about the creation of the world. What did God say after each phase of creation?

Now read Genesis 2:18. What did God say here?

Only when man was alone was it not good, and then God brought a remedy for man's aloneness. He created Eve to fill the emptiness in man and to be his helpmate. He saw man's need, and he met it. He is a good God.

- Then the enemy, Satan, enters the picture—and what did he do? Read Genesis 3:1.

He began to create doubt in Eve's heart regarding the goodness of God. *Did God really say…?* Satan is still doing that today. He begins to cause doubt in our hearts that God is good, that God loves us and desires the best for us. He causes us to doubt the Great Architect of our very being by whispering in our ear things like: "Has God truly said he will work all things for your good? Do you think he can remedy this situation? Don't be a fool. You're going to have to figure this one out by yourself, honey. Go ahead, eat that fruit of the world's solutions. You won't really die."

And the cycle starts again. We doubt God's goodness and his concern for us. We declare our independence from God by not trusting in his goodness to deliver us.

Our oldest daughter used to say to us, "I'll do it me-self, Daddy (or Mommy)."

Isn't that what we say to our heavenly Father? "Thank you very much. You just sit up there in heaven on a cloud with the Bible and all its flowery phrases. This is the real world. I'll figure this one out me-self."

We probably wouldn't state it exactly that way. We may even be sitting in church listening to a powerful sermon saying, "Amen, brother, preach on!"

We loudly proclaim we believe the Bible. The scary thing is, we really think we do believe it, but we never allow our belief to hit the streets and become reality.

As we leave the church building, we take up the blueprints of our lives in our own hands. We sit down at the drafting table of our days working feverishly on God's master plans, erasing, adding, tweaking, until we have made corrections we assume are beautiful and functional. However, when we hold the altered document up to the light, the etchings are not beautiful and functional at all. They are ugly, childish scribbling. We have snatched the blueprint of our lives away from the Great Architect—the only one who knows the master plan and the only one who can bring it to pass. We have told him by our actions that we do not want him to continue to draw the plans. It is taking too long. We are tired of waiting.

Besides that, the plans don't look as we had imagined them, so we are going to take over ourselves. "Thank you very much, I'll do it me-self, Daddy."

- In what ways have you decided to do things your way and ignored or rebelled against the Father's plans for your life?

For several years my husband and I directed a conference center. Each summer we would employ somewhere around twenty-five to thirty Christian young people, college age and older, to live at the camp and work as counselors and work crew. These were young people whose desire was to serve the Lord and glorify him. They loved Jesus, but we noted that they frequently had a problem with self-acceptance and self-esteem.

We began giving a psychological profile to all of our staff members at the beginning of the season. Sure enough—there it was—low self-image. The schedule was grueling, the work demanding, and inter-personal relationships so critical that we knew we needed to offer some help.

Psalm 139 became our constant companion. We required those dedicated young people, most of them from stable, loving, Christian families, to memorize the chapter in order to let the Scripture permeate their spirits.

- Read verses 1-6 of Psalm 139. What does God know about us?

God knows everything about us. We are vulnerable before him. He knows our thoughts, our unuttered words, when we sit down, when we get up. Does an architect not know every nook and cranny of a house? Just as a physical structure bears the touches and style of its architect, God's personal imprint is upon us.

- What makes you feel most vulnerable? Check the ones that apply.

    ___That he knows you intimately? (v. 1)

    ___That he knows your thoughts? (v. 2)

    ___That he knows all your ways? (v. 3)

    ___That he knows all the things you say—even the things you would like to say and don't? (v. 4)

    ___That he hems you in and puts limitations on you? (v. 5)

    ___That his hand is upon you? (v. 5)

In verses 7-12 the Word tells us because we are vulnerable before him, we try to flee.

We try to do it ourselves. "I'll do it me-self, thank you very much!" We try to shut him out of our lives. But there is nowhere we can go.

> Not into Heaven, for he is there. (v. 8)
>
> Not in the keeping place of the dead, for he is there as well. (v. 8)
>
> Not in the depths of the sea. (v. 9) (Jonah tried that - to no avail!)
>
> Not in the darkness, for his light exposes us. (vv. 10-11)

The Holy Spirit has been called the "Holy Hound of Heaven".

- Recall and record below a time when you tried to run from God and how the "Holy Hound of Heaven" hemmed you in and brought you back to himself.

Reading verses 13-16 reveals that the Great Architect has designed everything. He formed all my parts. He wove them together in my mother's womb. Verse 14 says I am fearfully and wonderfully made, and I should praise him for that. Praise him!? For my appearance? Absolutely. He formed you just the way he wanted you. He is the Great Architect.

- Is there anything about how God made you for which you cannot praise him?

Verse 16 is an interesting passage. The Scripture says that the Great Architect was watching my "unformed body," before I ever took shape. According to Strong's, the Hebrew word in this verse for "unformed body" is *golem,* which means "an unformed mass, such as an embryo." All the days ordained for me were written in his book before I ever was born, when I was simply an embryo in my mother's womb.

I heard an evangelist and Bible teacher, Manley Beasley, say years ago, "Victory is fulfilling what is written of you."

Victory is following the blueprints God has drawn up for our lives. That's God's will for you—to do what is written of you in his book.

God, the Great Architect, had already drawn up the blueprints for the millions of babies, which have been aborted in America. The Scripture tells us that those were not simply blobs of tissue, but embryos for whose lives blueprints had been drawn.

The Great Architect had the plans, the blueprints, of your life ready to go before you were even born. Building a life that is a sound structure is simply a matter of following the Great Architect's plans for you. The wise woman builds her house by beginning at the starting point— by consulting the Great Architect and trusting the blueprints he has ordained for her life.

- Meditate on Psalm 139:23-24.

  Search me (thoroughly), O God, and know my heart!

  Try me and know my thoughts.

  And see if there is any wicked or hurtful way in me,

  and lead me in the way everlasting" (Amp).

In the Hebrew, the language in which David originally prayed this prayer, the word for "search" is *chaqar,* which means "to penetrate, to examine intimately."

- Are you willing for the Great Architect of the universe and of your life to examine you intimately, to penetrate, and see if there is any hurtful or wicked way in you?

If you desire that, pray the two verses above before you consider this final question.

- *Building Tool* - Have you been angry or bitter with the Lord because you haven't liked the blueprints he has drawn up for your life? If you have been, write out a prayer below expressing your frustrations. That is what a great percentage of the Psalms are all about—David pouring out his heart, his hurt, his torment, and, yes, his complaints to the Lord. As the Psalmist did, ask the Lord's forgiveness for your independence, your doubt, your lack of trust in the blueprints he has drawn up for your life.

- *Small Group Discussion*: Perhaps you have not been angry about his plans for you, but you have been remiss in expressing praise. Do it now. Write a prayer or song or poem of thanksgiving below to him addressing him as the Great Architect of your life. Divide into groups of three and then share it with the group. Close in a prayer of encouragement for each other.

Chapter Four

The Blueprint – Father Knows Best

For we are God's workmanship, created in Christ Jesus to do good works, which God prepared in advance for us to do (Ephesians 2:10).

The Blueprint

Our church is currently in the process of building a worship center, classrooms and offices. The associate pastor, a former building contractor, is in charge of the new building. He filled the position of architect, designed the structure and drew up the blueprints. Many times I went into his office to see him hunched over his drafting table carefully scrutinizing the plans for the center. I watched him meticulously align and fit each detail in place for the needs of our church body. Our church puts on several productions a year and we need a stage with several different levels and good lighting. We hold conferences during the year, which requires more meeting space, more seating, and adequate bathroom facilities for large crowds. The kitchen required expanding. He knew the idiosyncrasies of our church fellowship, and thus knew exactly what should go into the plans.

The blueprints were then copied and put in the hands of the construction crew. As they began their work of interpreting the plans and each configuration became a physical reality, we would peer through the windows and marvel at the beauty of the emerging edifice from the raw materials of wood and steel and concrete. Occasionally the architect had to explain a direction or a detail to the workmen. Inspectors arrived unannounced and checked the work. Sometimes adjustments needed to be made.

The developing structure grew out of the intricate plans and schemes drawn by an architect who knew precisely where each pipe, each electrical line, each door and window needed to be placed. The architect could see in his mind's eye how he desired this construction to function and what he wanted it to look like. He foresaw the activities that would take place in the building he had so painstakingly designed. The people who would come and go and worship in the facility were a vision in his heart as he worked. He foresaw the worship that would ring out over the rafters and bring glory to the Father. He knew that people would come to know the Lord and be discipled as they passed through the adjoining classrooms. The offices that would be used for administrative work and counseling were formulated with an eye to where each piece of equipment would be placed, from the pastor's desk to the copy machine. He knew from the beginning how it would be used to further the Kingdom of God.

I think God must like blueprints. Throughout the Bible we find God giving plans to his people for their lives, a task, or a mission.

- Read Genesis 6:9-22. For what kind of structure is God giving a blueprint here?

For what purpose?

Why?

Why do you think God chose Noah? (See vs. 9.)

Do you think the phrase "a righteous man, blameless among the people of his time" meant that Noah was perfect?

Why or why not?

This description of Noah does not imply sinless perfection, but meant that his godly lifestyle was in sharp contrast to that of the culture around him. Noah was a man who walked with God, and God knew he could trust Noah to be obedient and follow directions.

God gave Noah very specific directions to build a strange structure, which would protect him and his family from a deluge that was to come. Noah didn't know exactly how it would occur, but he knew judgment was coming, and God was making provision for them. So Noah proceeded to follow the blueprint. Perhaps it didn't make sense to him. Perhaps he felt inadequate for the task. Surely his neighbors and acquaintances ridiculed him for building a huge boat miles from any size body of water? But Noah believed God and was obedient to follow the blueprint God gave him.

- Can God trust you to be obedient and follow his directions even when you don't understand and are bewildered at his leading?

The story of the life of Moses is a prime example of how God directs and protects those of his own whom he has chosen. The blueprint for Moses' life before the foundation of the earth was for him to be the deliverer of the children of Israel. Let's see how God orchestrated that plan to come about.

- Read Exodus 2 – 3:10. Write down the crisis points the Scriptures give us, the turning points, in Moses' life.

- Did Moses understand the scope of his "ministry" from the beginning?

- Write down crisis points, turning points, in your life, the time of your life they occurred (not dates, but seasons – i.e. childhood, teenager), whether you believed God or not, and what resulted.

The Crisis	Season of Your Life	Believed God?	Result

- Could it be the blueprint God has for you is working itself out through the twists and turns of your life?

- What did Moses have to do to follow that blueprint?

- What must you do to follow the blueprint for your life?

Just as God gave Noah a blueprint for the ark and there was a blueprint for Moses' life, God gave Moses an exact blueprint for the place where his spirit would reside with his people—the Tabernacle.

- Turn to and peruse Exodus 25-30. Note how precise the instructions are for the Tabernacle, the furnishings and the garments for the priests. Why do you think God was so meticulous in his specifications for the Tabernacle and its furnishings?

The Tabernacle is a fascinating and copious study of its own, but suffice it to say here that each measurement, each piece of fabric, each color, every design in the Tabernacle had a distinct meaning and function. Some designs foreshadowed Jesus and his death, some depicted the glory of God, some envisioned the Holy Spirit, but each project within the Tabernacle, and later the Temple, had to be followed precisely in order for the intent and purpose of God to be complete. I think if I had been one of the artisans involved in the building of the Tabernacle, I would have been apprehensive about having the responsibility of crafting the instruments exactly right.

When we were in Jerusalem several years ago, we went to an institute that is remaking the instruments to go in the Temple. They believe the Temple will be rebuilt when Jesus comes back to the earth and the Jewish form of worship will be reinstated. Scholars differ on that premise, but we were interested to note how precise all the preparations were and how closely they attempted to remake them according to Scripture.

- In Chapter 25 of Exodus we find the specifications for the ark, the table of shewbread and the lampstand. Choose one of them and take a stab at drawing it out below. Don't look it up in a commentary before you draw your own rendition. Note how precise the directions are.

Like the ark, Moses' life and the Tabernacle, the Bible gives us many examples of how God coordinated the details of the lives of those through whom he desired to be effective in the Kingdom. As we discussed in Chapter three, God has exact plans drawn up for our lives as well. Scripture assures us that we are no accident. Our heavenly Father knit our unformed body like a beautiful tapestry, each thread intricately woven into the masterpiece for a unique purpose.

God, the Great Architect, has written the days of our lives even before we were born (Psalm 139:15-16). God knew us when we were in our mother's womb and set us apart to serve him according to his plans to prosper us and give us hope and a future (Jeremiah 1:5 and Jeremiah 29:11). He chose us before the foundation of the earth (Ephesians 1:4). We are his workmanship created to be effective in the Kingdom (Ephesians 2:10). The Greek word there for "workmanship" is *poiayma*. That is the word from which we get "poem," a work of art. You are a work of art that God has created in Jesus to do good works.

Sometimes it is difficult for me to wrap my mind around these concepts. God had *me* in mind before the foundation of the earth? He set *me* apart for himself? He had plans to prosper *me*—to give *me* a future and a hope? *I* am his "work of art?"

- *Building Tool* – Perhaps you too have difficulty grasping the fact that God was thinking about you before the foundation of the earth. It will be helpful to get these Scriptures into our heart so they will penetrate our spirit with that truth. Write them out below and choose one to memorize, one you don't already know. Or you could memorize more than one. Be prepared to quote the verses you chose next time your small group meets.

Psalm 139:15-16

Jeremiah 1:5

Jeremiah 29:11

Ephesians 1:4

Ephesians 2:10

I worked with and taught youth for many years and the most frequently asked question was this: "How do I know God's will for my life?" That's really what we are talking about here, isn't it? How do I know what God's plan, his blueprint, for my life is? How do I know how to follow it? What steps do I take? Where do I find the answers? How do I hear God?

The Sound of His Voice

Like Noah and the building of the ark, Moses as he became the deliverer of the children of Israel and God's people as they followed the pattern to build the Tabernacle, we are responsible to follow the instructions God gives us for our lives. The answer I gave young people when they asked that ubiquitous question, "How do I know God's will for my life?" was this: "If you will do what God tells you to do on a daily basis, at the end of six months, or a year, or five years, or ten years, you will be in God's will."

It was a very simple answer—one that was sometimes too simple to satisfy their questioning minds. Some would come back with what I call "yeah but" theology. "Yeah, but, what if .... "

"Yeah, that's true, but ... " and off they would go on some tangent.

But sometimes I would see the light bulb turn on in a teenager's eyes, and I knew they got it.

"You mean, all I have to do is listen to God daily and do what he says, and I am following God's will?"

"You've got it."

"That's all I have to do?'

"Umm-hmm. Follow him daily and he will guide you into his will. God is more eager for you to know his will for your life than you are to find it. He will show you. Just listen to his voice."

As I approached my senior year in high school, I desperately wanted to go to college. All my friends were preparing to do so, but there were no plans to further my education in my future. My family was barely able to provide shelter and food for us, much less pay for college. But I believed God wanted me to go to college, and not only that, I believed he had turned my heart to a particular, private, Christian college. I believed it was his will for me.

Day by day I continued to trust him, even though it appeared futile. I proceeded with my schoolwork, doing the best I knew how to do. My grades were good, and I was involved in many extra-curricular activities.

One morning the high school counselor called me into his office to ask me why I had not yet applied to go to a university. I told him that there were no funds to attend college, but that I would very much like to go. He asked me where I would like to go. Taking a big breath, I bravely blurted out the name of the university I felt God leading me toward.

The counselor set up an appointment for me to take a battery of tests at this university. There was a major problem, however. We had no car. I had no way to get there. But, again, following God's leadership on a daily basis, I accepted the appointment and rode the bus to the town in which the university was located. I took the tests, was shown around campus by a student with whom I later became good friends, met the president of the university, in whose office I got a job the next year, and, yes, received a scholarship to go to college. It was at this university that I met my husband.

You see, following God's leadership on a daily basis takes you to God's eventual will for your life. At any point along the way, I could have thrown up my hands and exclaimed, "There is no way! I'll just get a good job and stay in my home town and work." But it was God's will for me to go to college. His plan is not for everyone to go to college, but it was for me. I was to further my education and prepare for ministry. As I followed him day by day, he revealed it bit by bit.

We think that finding God's will for our life needs to be surrounded by fireworks and a big, deep, booming voice. Or we need to have an experience like Paul had on the road to Damascus where he met Jesus. He literally fell to the ground, blinded. We keep looking for that experience that knocks our socks off. But it is really the opposite most of the time.

- Read I Kings 19:11-12. Name the natural phenomena that Elijah experienced as he waited on the Lord. (1)

(2)

(3)

What did God's voice sound like when Elijah finally heard it?

- What does God's voice sound like when you hear it? Is it loud and booming or soft and gentle?

- Read Isaiah 30:21. Now to put it in context, read the whole chapter, and contrast verse 21 with verses 10-11. How did God's voice come to His people? (v. 21)

- How did it come to the enemies of His people? (vv. 30-31)

- Look up and read the following Scriptures. Document the occasion, the reason for God's speaking at the time, and what it sounded like.

Scripture	Occasion	Reason	Sound of His voice
Genesis 3:8-9			
Job 40:9			

Psalm 29

John 10:4

There are many Scriptures on the voice of God. As I did this word study, it seemed to me that at those times when God's majesty is being displayed or he is coming against the enemies of his people; his voice is loud and booming like thunder, or like the rush of mighty waters. But when he speaks to his people, it seems to be soft and gentle. God's voice and direction comes to us in many forms, but it has been my experience it is that quiet, still, small voice. It is rarely loud, or harsh, or intruding. It "nudges" us to do this or say that.

When I was a young bride, my godly mother-in-law taught me that those "nudges" to call someone, or write a card, or stop by a friend's house, are often the Holy Spirit's direction. "Whether you turn to the right or to the left, your ears will hear a voice behind you saying, 'This is the way; walk in it.' " (Isaiah 30:21).

- Can you think of a time that you followed God's voice day by day and ultimately found yourself in what he desired for you?

Hearing God's Voice in the Word

God, as the Great Architect of our lives, will bring correction, discipline and encouragement through his voice in the Word. He will keep us on target as we seek to interpret the blueprints of our lives.

God's voice will always agree with the written Word. Early in our ministry, a friend revealed to us that he was having an extra-marital affair. He proceeded to tell us God had told him that it was permissible for him to pursue the affair. *Somebody* had given him permission, but it sure wasn't God.

In the ensuing years the number of times that individuals have come to us and expressed the same sentiments is incalculable. Satan is a master of deceit, and if he can convince a person that sin is okay, he has won a major battle. If the Word prohibits an action and calls it sin, that is exactly what it is. No matter how we rationalize it, if it does not line up with Scripture, it is not God. God's voice will agree with the principles in the written Word every time.

- Have you ever rationalized your behavior by claiming God said it was permissible for you to engage in an action in the special circumstances in which you found yourself, but you knew Scripture taught otherwise? What were the circumstances and what did you do about it?

We have to know the Word, however, in order to discern whether we are straying from the blueprint. We need to have a daily time with the Lord, reading the Word and listening for his voice. And as much as we might like to get around it, all through Scripture we find that early in the morning seems to be the best time.

- Read Psalm 5:1-3. When was the prayer of the psalmist offered and heard?

- Read Psalm 57:8. When did David praise the Lord with his instruments?

- Read Mark 1:35. What time of day did Jesus get alone to be with God?

It's not that we cannot pray and listen to God at other times during the day – in fact, the Scripture also talks about the night watches, and praying without ceasing, but the early morning seems to be the prime time that the great men and women of God sought Him. Bruce Wilkinson says in his book, *Secrets of the Vine,* "… I have yet to find a respected spiritual leader throughout history who had devotions at night. Unless you get up early, you're unlikely to break through to a deeper relationship with God."

That is a strong assertion, and I am not sure that blanket statement can be applied generally, but it does indicate how important some great men and women of God throughout history have felt the early morning hours with the Lord are.

However true those statements are, we can get legalistic about a daily quiet time, if we're not careful. We can grit our teeth, set our alarm clocks (after being up too late the night before), drag ourselves out of bed, read a ten minute devotional and not get a thing out of it.

One of our favorite speakers at the retreat center we managed was Major Ian Thomas. Major Thomas is the founder of Torchbearer Ministries in England, and has written many books, that have become classics in the Christian realm, *The Saving Life of Christ, If I Perish, I Perish* and *The Mystery of Godliness.*

One morning around the breakfast table one of the conferees asked Major Thomas, "What do you think about quiet times?"

In his quick, sharp style, Major Thomas shot back at him, "Idolatry," as he continued eating his breakfast.

You could hear gasps from those around the table. Then it got very quiet. Major Thomas looked up and began to chuckle, "Unless, that is, your sole purpose is to be with Jesus."

We do not have a quiet time so we can check it off our spiritual shopping list. It is to hear God's voice—to be sure we are sticking with the blueprint.

- *Building Tool* – Would you be willing to commit to a daily quiet time for at least three weeks to listen for God's voice? It takes twenty-one days to form a habit. Get a good devotional book, classics such as Oswald Chamber's *My Utmost For His Highest* or *Streams in the Desert,* L. B. Cowman. Or pick up a more contemporary book like *Secrets of the Vine* by Bruce Wilkinson, *Growing Strong in the Seasons of Life* by Charles Swindoll, or *The Mystery of Majesty* by Dennis Jernigan. The Christian bookstores are full of good devotionals. A devotional Bible, such as the Women's Devotional Bible, is also helpful. In addition to a good devotional aid, acquire some kind of diary or journal to record your journey, even a spiral notebook will do. But set aside some time every morning to read the word and listen to God. Write down what you think you hear him saying to you. Write down Scriptures that "jump" out at you. Write down your prayers. Through the years I have tried all kinds of journals, books and methods for having a quiet time. Don't get crazy with it. Don't beat yourself up if you miss a few mornings. Just start again, and you will soon get in the habit. Especially if you have small children, it is going to be difficult, but ask the Lord to help you.

I try to remember every morning when I wake up before I even swing my legs over the edge of the bed and hit the floor, to offer myself to the Lord for that day. "Lord, what do you want me to do today? I am your willing vessel to do in and through me anything you desire. Help me to perform the menial chores and tasks I have confronting me with joy and an attitude of gratitude. Give me a thankful heart. Help me to see opportunities to be Jesus to those around me today. Help me accept phone calls and people in my life today not as interruptions, but as divine appointments."

Then I get up and continue to pray as I go to the kitchen to make a pot of coffee. I turn on some praise music, and after the coffee brews, I sit down in my favorite chair and read and listen for God's voice. Don't make it complicated. Just be faithful.

- *Small Group Discussion*: (1) Quote the Scriptures to each other you were to memorize this week: Psalm 139:15-16; Jeremiah 1:5; Jeremiah 29:11, Ephesians 1:4 and/or Ephesians 2:10. (2) Discuss what God's voice sounds like to each of the members of the group. (3) Share with each other some of your struggles and victories you have experienced in your daily time with the Lord. Discuss what God said to you this week, Scriptures that spoke to you, answered prayer. End with prayer for each other.

Chapter Five

Rock Your Foundation or Your Foundation The Rock?

*Through skillful and godly Wisdom is a house (a life, a home, a family)
built and by understanding it is established (on a sound and good foundation) and by knowledge
shall the chambers (of its every area) be filled with all precious and pleasant riches (Proverbs
24:3-4 Amplified).*

The Foundation

We have discovered that we need a good architect before we even start building

our houses, our lives, our homes, our families. Our architect is the Great Architect of the

Universe, the Lord God Almighty, and he has the blueprints for our lives in hand. Now we are

ready to proceed with our houses. The first item on the agenda is the foundation.

- What does the above Scripture say about laying a foundation and building our lives, homes and families?

How and from what sources do most of us garner understanding for our foundational values? Unfortunately, most of us depend upon culture and society or tradition or logic to dictate to us the standards by which we build our lives and our marriages.

- Read Proverbs 1:5-7; 2:1-11; 4:5-7; Psalm 119:104. From where do we get wisdom and understanding?

- According to the Scriptures we have read, how important is wisdom and understanding to building our lives?

- What are some of the rewards and results you see in these Scriptures from gaining wisdom and understanding?

I believe that every one of us as followers of Jesus comes to the point in our lives when we have to decide whether or not we are going to believe the Word of God—whether or not we are going to base our lives on Scripture. There is a crisis of belief at every fork in the road when we must choose to go with what Scripture teaches or follow the mores of society, culture and tradition. Much of the time the pain of our emotions or sentimentalism shouts louder in our hearts than the truth of God's Word. We proceed to lay a foundation of good provision, or college degrees and education, or solid ancestry, or mutual respect, or even being good church members. We desperately attempt to lay a foundation of falling madly in love. According to Hollywood and our society, being passionately in love seems to be the only foundation. It *is* nice and feels good, but is that the foundation, which will stand when tough times come? Does a wise woman build her home and life on these shifting values? The tangibles that we can see with our eyes capture us, and the faith that is required to believe God is buried under an avalanche of cars, homes, boats, piano lessons, football games and church activities.

- Can you think of any major decisions you made in your life and based those decisions not on Scripture, but on society's values or tradition or logic? What were they?

- What were the results?

- In what ways would your life be different if you had asked for God's wisdom, believed Him and been obedient to His plan?

- *Building Tool* – Let's stop right now before we proceed and ask God to forgive us if we have built our lives on the foundation of the values of society, culture and tradition instead of the wisdom and understanding we glean from his Word. We have all fallen victim to the philosophy of the world at one time or another. To repent means to turn the other direction and change our behavior. Repent and ask the Lord to forgive you. Express to him that you desire to be a wise woman and are going to trust his Word and begin to build on the foundation that He has provided for us. Now we are ready to study about that foundation.

Let's see what Scripture says about a solid foundation. The Scripture tells us that through wisdom and understanding our home is built and established on a sound foundation. It is from Scripture that we gain understanding, so let's look at what the Scriptures say the foundation is.

- In 1 Corinthians. 3:11, what do you find is the foundation?

1 Corinthians. 3:11 is simple and self-explanatory. Jesus Christ is the foundation. Jesus is the only sure foundation. There is no other.

- What function does a foundation perform?

I remember the first time we went out to look at the freshly poured foundation of that big, two-story house we were building. I was amazed. I looked at my husband and asked him, "Has the foundation been poured correctly? Will it support the house?"

He assured me it was adequate. It didn't look to me like it would be, but I had to trust our architect. I had to trust our builder. I had to believe he was skilled in his abilities and knew what kind of structure the house needed in order to stand securely through the years and through all kinds of weather.

We can look all day long at the foundation of a house, adamantly declaring our belief that it will hold up the building, but until we start putting bricks and mortar to it, building our houses upon what has been laid, we have not actually put our trust in it. That is exactly what we do when we place our trust in Jesus. It is not merely mental assent. It is not simply believing. It is placing the burden of the whole structure, our entire lives, on the foundation. The Amplified Bible says that to believe means to trust in, cling to, rely on. That is much more than mental belief. It means that when the crises come, and we can be assured that they will come, we trust in, cling to and rely on Jesus to be active in our lives.

"Jesus is the head of our household," is not just a sentimental phrase to throw around hoping everything will work out for the best. It is an active, vital, vibrant belief that God is keeping our foundation sure and strong.

- Turn in your Bible to Matthew 7:24-27 and read that passage. Here we find the familiar story regarding the wise and foolish builders.

- What are the two foundations spoken of in the text?

As I write this, I have the little childhood song running around in my mind about the foolish man building his house upon the sand. The rains came down, and the floods came up, and the house on the sand went "kerplunk!" But the wise man built his house upon the rock and when the rains came down and the floods came up, the house on the rock stayed firm. That little song is good theology.

In the next chapter we are going to look at this passage more closely, but for now I want to look primarily at the foundation. Sand is a symbolic term in these verses for a foundation upon which we might build our homes that is shifting, unstable, unsteady and unsure.

- What are some contemporary items you think a foundation of sand might symbolize?

- What might be the foundation of "rock?"

The two houses represent the lives of two men. Both men were busy building their lives.

I imagine both houses looked wonderful on the outside. They both probably contained the latest technology of their day, beautifully landscaped, and perhaps presented gorgeous views. But there was a big difference in these two structures, and that big difference was the foundation. One was built on sand—the other on rock.

Our middle daughter and her husband built an imposing house a few years ago, situated on a hill with a magnificent view over rolling pastures and trees. The sunrises and sunsets from the vantage point of their house are breathtaking. The native stone and shutters on the windows blend in beautifully with the landscape. The details, trim and furnishings in the house reflect excellent taste. However, after only a few months, cracks began to appear in the walls and ceiling. The baseboards began to pull away from the sheet rock. The roof began to leak where there were defects. There was a flaw in the foundation. Now, they are in the process of redoing the foundation in order to save the house. The cost will probably be as much as one-third of the initial value of the entire structure. The soil in their area is sandy, and it shifts. A builder must be skilled in pouring a good foundation on this type of soil, but their builder poured a faulty foundation. It is proving costly to this young couple in the end.

- In what ways does your house/home look "fine" on the exterior?

- Have you noticed any "cracks" in your home because of a faulty foundation?

- Which foundation is your house built upon?

The Storms

All was fine for a period of time. Their lives went on as usual with both families enjoying their new houses. Then the storms came.

- Looking again at the Matthew 7:24-27 passage, upon which house did the rains fall?

- Upon which house did the floods descend?

- Upon which house did the winds blow?

Storms descended upon both houses. One house did not fall, because it was founded upon the rock. The other house fell because it was not founded upon the rock, but upon the sand. Jesus adds, "...and great was its fall."

- What storms has your house been through? (Take your time and be specific.)

- Did your house stay firm or did it go "kerplunk?"

My husband and I were privileged to travel to Israel a few years ago. Seeing with our physical eyes the roads, valleys and paths Jesus walked enabled us to see with our spiritual eyes some of the Bible passages with new vision.

Parts of Israel are barren, dry and dusty. One can imagine when the rains come how they must create raging streams of water cascading down the *wadis* (gullies), over the valleys and hillsides.

We were not in Israel during rainy season, but we did experience a phenomenon called the *sharqia*. The *sharqia* is an easterly wind, which comes up suddenly and blows with a ferocity difficult to describe. Now I understand what the Scripture means when it says, "The winds blew and <u>beat</u> against the house." I awoke during the middle of the night hearing the *sharqia* blowing in—wondering if our little bungalow on the Sea of Galilee was going to stand firm. The winds howled and beat against the house. It whistled frantically through the palm trees outside our patio door.

I do not know whether the houses in the parable were in the barren Judean wilderness where the torrents of water rush down the *wadis*, or around the Sea of Galilee where the *sharqia* blows with all its ferocious strength. Whichever is the case, I have a new appreciation for this parable. Each builder had a structure, which appeared on the surface to be secure. It was only when the storms came that the true nature of the building was revealed. Each house appeared to be sturdy enough until the storms beat upon them.

Do we not find this true in life? It is only when the storms come that the true strength of the house, the life, is revealed.

- Does the Scripture say, "<u>If</u> the storms come?" Write out what the verse says:

Dear friend, the storms are going to come. Your "house", your life, your family are going to experience the storms of life. Your storms will not be the same storms the Lord allows to come my way. I have discovered that the Great Architect allows only particular storms, which pattern themselves exactly after the blueprints he has drawn up for my life.

The storms are precisely what we need to polish the beautiful wood that God is putting in our houses, to sand the rough edges and corners in the house. They are like the unannounced inspector who shows up and points out adjustments that need to be made. The inspector simply reveals faults that are present. In the same manner, storms reveal where our homes need work. We may not even be aware of the changes that need attention in our lovely houses, but the Great Architect is very aware. He allows the rain to fall and the wind to beat against our house to make us aware of what He already knows. He knows just where to erase, change a dimension, sand and chip, cut away and polish to conform us to the image of Jesus.

Our praise and worship leader was for many years a custom homebuilder. His eye is so accurate that he can tell by merely looking at a beam or a piece of trim if it is out of line. Our heavenly Father knows precisely what needs to be brought back into line in our lives. His erasing, changing dimensions, sanding, chipping, cutting away and polishing us will not be comfortable.

Likewise being in the storm is uncomfortable. It is even more than that. Sometimes it hurts. It is painful. It is frightening at times. It shakes the whole structure. Sometimes you begin to wonder if the foundation is going to stand.

One spring during tornado season in East Texas where we directed a Christian retreat and conference center, the clouds in the sky began to bubble and brew up the dark gray-green color that those of us who live in "tornado alley" recognized all too well. The rain pelted down on my car in sheets. I could hardly see to drive home through the streaks of lightning, which flashed one after another. It was the sensation of having the flash of a camera go off in your face over and over again. I was concerned because one of our daughters was at a track meet, the other two were at our home, which was glass all along the back of the house. I never saw the funnel cloud, but when I arrived home and told our girls to take cover, the phone was ringing. It was our secretary down the road at the conference center office telling me that a tornado just went through and that the roof to the dormitory was gone.

As soon as the rain let up enough for us to get in the car and travel the short distance from our house to the lodge, we ventured outside. We were not able to get very far, however. Trees lay across the little oil dirt road blocking our path. We got out of the car and climbed over them to walk up to the dormitory. I shall never forget that sight. The roof was indeed gone, but when the tornado ripped it from the building, all the electrical and air conditioning systems collapsed inward. Beds and mattresses were strewn through the woods. Chairs from the meeting room lay mangled and in every imaginable position. The piano was wet, but remained in its original position, with the hymnbook open on the bookrack. Games were tossed here and there. One of our constituents was in the building at the time preparing for a weekend retreat and received a painful, but not serious, blow to the head. However, the foundation remained, and we were able to rebuild the dormitory, better than ever, on that original foundation. The period of rebuilding took several months, but it was relatively simple, because the foundation was strong.

That's how it is when we encounter storms in our lives. The situation may appear to be a mess. It may be painful. We may not like it. But if the foundation is strong and right, we can rebuild and our lives will be stronger and better than ever.

Once during a storm, when the winds were beating against our house and the floods were rising, I was whining and complaining. I asked the question, "Why me?"

A godly friend looked me straight in the eyes and said, "Why not you?"

- What does Scripture have to say about complaining and whining? (See Numbers 11:1; 14:27; 1 Corinthians 10:10; Philippians. 2:14-15.)

- Read Numbers 12:1-10. What were the consequences of Miriam's complaining?

- Why do you think God hates complaining?

I have a friend who calls it "weenie-whining." I don't believe you could find that phrase in a Bible concordance, but I love the terminology! The Bible calls it "murmuring," but perhaps "weenie-whining" is a more easily understood contemporary term that describes this problem of grumbling and complaining to us. I think God hates "weenie-whining" because when we fall into this bad habit, we are shaking our fist in the face of God and saying, "I don't approve of the way you are handling my life. I don't like the way you made me. I don't like the leadership you have placed over me. I would rather be doing something else or living somewhere else. You are not a good Father."

- Have you ever asked God, "Why me?"
- Turn to Romans 9:20-21. What does that Scripture say is God's answer to that question?

Why not me, indeed? Why not you? God loves us enough to allow our houses to be tested by the storms of life to see if they will stand—to see if they are solidly built upon the rock of Jesus Christ. He wants to see if there are any cracks in our foundation.

Both families experienced storms. The house on the sure foundation encountered the same storms that the one on the shifting foundation encountered. The house on the shifting foundation fell, but the one on the sure foundation remained steadfast. It all had to do with the foundation.

A couple of days before Christmas a few years ago, a car accident occurred on an icy farm road outside our town. Driving one of the vehicles was the young adult daughter of the associate pastor, who was my boss at the time. It was one of those freaky accidents where the victim appeared to be barely injured, but she was killed. As the car fishtailed crazily on the ice, her temple was crushed on the side of the window. She died instantly.

I shall never forget her dad's vibrant spirit at the funeral. He bounded up to the pulpit and began the funeral the same way he opened every Sunday morning service with, "This is the day the Lord hath made. Let us rejoice and be glad in it!" And his comment as he greeted those at the funeral, "We have hit bottom, but the bottom is solid rock!"

"On Christ the solid rock I stand, all other ground is sinking sand." That old hymn, *The Solid Rock,*[1] became reality to that precious family on a dreary, snowy, wintry day when the storms beat against their house, but their foundation remained secure.

Building on the foundation of Jesus Christ is not just commitment to a church, or a

---

[1] Bradbury, William B. and More, Edward, *The Hymnal for Worship & Celebration*, (Waco, Texas, Word Music, 1986), 404.

program, or a pastor—or even in simply believing in God. James 2:19 reveals that even the demons believe in God and tremble. It is in laying a sound foundation on the solid rock of the Lord Jesus. Trusting in the fact that there is no other way, no other payment for our sin except through the redeeming blood of Christ. Establishing a personal relationship with Jesus.

Nobody starts out building a life intending to fail. We all plan to be successful in building our lives, our marriages, our homes, and our families. However, something happens along the way, and we realize we have not gained the understanding of which the Scripture speaks to build on a good and solid foundation. The storms come and the foundation on the sand begins to shift.

- *Building Tool* – (1) As you have gone through this chapter you may have realized that your house is built on shifting sand. You may have tried to build upon a foundation of romantic love, only to find the emotions waning. Or upon the fact that you or your spouse is a good provider, or that you and your spouse have the same goals in life. Would you be willing to pray and tell the Lord Jesus that you want to build upon the solid foundation, which is already laid – that of Christ Himself? Write out your prayer expressing your desire to make him the foundation of your life, your home, your family.

(2) Would you be willing to share your desire this week with your spouse?

(3) Most of you doing this study have probably already made Jesus your Lord and Savior, but there may be just a small area in your foundation that has a crack. Perhaps you are trying to run things yourself in the area of finances or in guiding your children or in submission to your husband. Ask the Lord to "shore up" the foundation and give you the understanding of a wise woman in whatever area in your home you feel is weak. Write out your prayer:

(4) Have you been guilty of murmuring and complaining—"weenie weining"—about how God has been handling your life, how he has made you, how he is using you or where you are at this point in your life? Pray and ask God to forgive you. You may be in the midst of a storm at this very moment. Tell him you trust him and what he is doing in your life. Write your prayer out below. Be specific.

- *Small Group Discussion*: Divide into groups of three or four. (1) If you have never committed your life to Jesus, there's no better time than right now. Tell your group that during this study you have realized you need to come to Jesus – not just church membership or simply believing in God, but a vital personal relationship with Him. Ask the women in your group to help you. It's important that you reach out to them and confess Jesus with your mouth. The Scripture says that "With the heart man believes and with the mouth confession is made unto salvation." Allow your group to pray with you. (2) If you are already a follower of Jesus, share with your group what the circumstances were when you committed your life to Jesus. In other words, share your testimony with your group. How old were you? Where were you physically? How did you respond? Who helped you—a pastor, a parent, a friend? Pray together and thank and praise him for calling you to be one of his children. Thank him for the steady, secure, stable, sure and solid foundation, which is holding up your household. (3) Share with the group if you are struggling with murmuring and complaining— "weenie-whining"—about how God is handling your life. Be specific where appropriate. Ask your Christian sisters to pray for you. (4) It may be you are in the midst of a storm at this very moment. Would you be willing to share with your group what you are going through and ask them to pray for you? I was leading a conference in a church in a large metropolitan area teaching on the broken heart. A lady performed in a drama portraying a woman whose husband was having an affair. As I moved through my teaching, she began to weep uncontrollably. Meeting in their small groups afterwards, her friends discovered to their shock that the very part she played in the drama was indeed what she was facing in real life. Much healing was accomplished as those Christian ladies gathered and prayed for her. Don't be fearful of being vulnerable. That is when healing takes place. (5) Pray with each other asking the Lord to grant you wisdom and understanding as to how to build your lives, families and homes on a sure foundation.

Chapter Six

Bricks or Sticks?

"Therefore every one who hears these words of mine and puts them into practice is like a wise

man who built his house upon the rock" (Matthew 7:24 NIV).

A Hearing Test

Jesus makes this provocative statement at the conclusion of the Sermon on the Mount

before he relates the parable of the wise and foolish man. Did you notice the "hearing test" --

"everyone who *hears?*"

I looked up the word "hear" in Strong's concordance and guess what it means? It means "to hear." I expected to find that it had a deep, theological, hidden meaning, but it simply means to hear.

Have you ever said to your children, "Did you hear me?" Why did you say that? Was it because they were hearing-impaired or was it perhaps because you suspected that they were not listening to you? Perhaps they were distracted by something else like the television or a friend, but because they were not doing what you asked them to do, you realized your child was not really hearing. If we do not put into practice what we have heard, have we really heard?

- Have you heard God tell you something you should be doing, but you are not doing it?

  What is it?

- Is it because you didn't really "hear" him, or because you have chosen to be disobedient?

- Read Chapters 5-7 in the Book of Matthew. I know this is a lot of reading, but it is the Sermon on the Mount and is important in order to get the context of Jesus' remarks. As he ends this famous sermon, what serious charge does Jesus issue to us?

We find in this passage on the Sermon on the Mount a wealth of instructions—solid, sturdy bricks—for godly living. There we find the Beatitudes. We read about our responsibilities to our fellowman—being salt and light, the importance of forgiveness, no adultery, no false vows, no retaliation, the second mile, loving your enemies, and no judgment. Instructions regarding our relationship with the Father are included—prayer, true treasure, and faith. Then in verse 13 of chapter 7, Jesus begins to bring it all to a close by talking about a series of twos. Read verses 13-20.

- What are the "twos" about which he is speaking? Write them out below.

- What is the narrow gate? (See John 10:7)

- What is the wide gate?

- What is the narrow road?

- What is the broad road?

- What is a good tree? (See James 3:12 and Luke 6:43-45.)

- What is a bad tree?

- What is good fruit? (See Galatians 5:22-23.)

- What is bad fruit? (See Galatians 5:19-12.)

We stand at a crossroads now. We can choose to go Jesus' way, the narrow gate and road, which is life and produces a good tree and good fruit. Or we can go the way of the world, which is broad and looks good, but is a bad tree and produces bad, rotten fruit.

If we use the building materials of the world in our marriage (sticks), the house may look good on the outside for awhile. We may appear to have a good relationship with our spouse and a successful business. We are active in the PTO, give to charity and are leaders in the community. We are members of the country club, play golf, enjoy good health, are tanned and prosperous. We are active in our local church. Our kids attend the children's and youth activities. We are officers in the ladies auxiliary, and we go to Women of Faith every year. Our husbands even attend Promise Keepers with the men's group at church. The fruit appears good, but upon closer examination, something is wrong. It is sour or rotten on the inside.

Have you ever bought a piece of fruit that looked beautiful and colorful on the outside, only to find it mealy or sour when you bit into it? Disappointing, isn't it? Here where we live in the mountains of northern New Mexico, it is hard to find good fruit. We shop diligently at the super markets, pressing tenderly on the peaches or tomatoes hoping we have found a good specimen. Occasionally we see a label on a piece of fruit that lets us know that it was grown in a particular spot that produces tasty produce. We eagerly snatch it up, hoping that when we get it home and cut into it, the fruit will indeed be sweet and delicious. But we never know until we put it to the litmus test of taste. Until we cut into it and look on the inside, we don't really know if it is good fruit or bad.

It's the same with the Christian walk. Until we are tested, we don't really know if we are bearing good or bad fruit.

- *Building Tool* - Is there anything in your home that looks like good fruit on the outside, but is rotten on the inside? Ask the Lord to reveal to it you. You may not even be aware of it up to this point. Go to your kitchen right now and pick up a piece of fruit. (If you don't have any fruit in your home at the moment, buy some at the store the next time you go and do this little experiment.) Take a bite. Is it sweet, juicy and delicious? Or is it mealy and dry, or sour, or even worse, rotten? Maybe it is bruised. How does the piece of fruit compare with your walk with the Lord?

- How are you doing regarding going through the narrow gate and traveling the narrow road? Are you staying on the narrow way? Or are you trying to jump over ditches between the narrow way and the broad way? What happens when you try to do both?

We might say something like, "Now, wait a minute, I believe in God, but I don't have to be a fanatic, do I? It's not necessary to go overboard on this Jesus stuff. Going to church once a week is a good family thing to do. It makes the upcoming week go so much better. The Sunday School classes are beneficial for the children, and the couple's class is a good fellowship group for us. But we live in the real world and need to use our common sense, don't we?"

A young woman came up to me recently after a worship service at our church, and I could tell from the smile on her face and the tears in her eyes that the Lord had been dealing with her. This lady is very visible in our community, owns two thriving businesses and is active in our church. She has been a Christian for a long time, but is experiencing a growth spurt in her faith. God has taken her through some major difficulties in the past three years. Her son was driving a vehicle after recently getting his driver's license, lost control of the car, and his friend was killed. A drawn-out litigation process followed. Doctors discovered a lump in her neck. She ran for mayor of our little village and experienced slander during the campaign. God is "shaking her cage." She has been taking tentative, cautious steps toward abandoning herself completely to Jesus.

As she approached me, these were her words, "God is telling me that I need to be as passionate about him as I am about some of the other things in which I am involved. I've always been afraid of being labeled a fanatic, but it's time for me to step out."

- What is your definition of a fanatic?"

I heard someone say one time that a fanatic is someone who believes something more strongly than I do. Most of us can relate to the fear of being labeled a fanatic, and the religious variety seems to scare us more than any other kind.

- Have you ever been a fanatic about anything?

  What was it?

- Was it a positive or a negative?

- Would being a fanatic about your marriage, spouse and children be a positive or negative?

  Why or why not?

There was a point in our marriage when we found ourselves on the brink of divorce. We were deeply involved in ministry. It was a dark place to be. I had allowed my affections to be drawn away from my husband by another man. I was entangled in a web of emotions, deceit and betrayal. I strayed from the best for my life and our marriage, but my commitment to the Lord was such that I could not entertain the thought of divorce. I did not want to drag my children through what I had experienced in my family of origin.

As discussed in Chapter Two, I felt marriage was a covenant not to be broken. I was being a fanatic about the marriage covenant, even though I allowed my emotions to stray for awhile. My husband forgave me, and we began to work on our relationship.

The reconciliation process took time, but today we have a wonderful relationship. Our daughters were able to grow up in a stable, secure home. Being a fanatic and staking my life on Scripture was worth it. I believed God would restore our marriage, and he did. I felt foolish at times, but God was faithful and the bricks of the Word of God proved strong and held our home together. I remember as a teen-ager hearing an evangelist preach a sermon on "Being a Fool For Christ's Sake." The concept made a profound impact on me. I'd never heard anything like that before.

- Read 1 Corinthians 4:10. Do you think God really expects us to be "fools for Christ's sake?" Why or why not?

- Would you consider being a "fool for Christ's sake" the same as being a fanatic? Why or why not?

People who make a difference are different. Why are we terrified of being different? I don't want to live my life blending in with the crowd and being traditional and status quo. I want to make a difference for Jesus and his glory. I want my marriage to be light in a world of darkness, salt to those who need spice in their relationships, a city set on a hill, good fruit. The world is desperate to know people who truly live by what they profess to believe.

My growing-up years were sad ones. My dad drank heavily. Mom was weighed down with simply making enough money to put a roof over our heads and feed us. I decided that I was going to make it somehow, someway. I accepted the Lord my freshman year in high school, and began to realize that he would make a way for me. I started praying for a Christian husband and family. One of my closest friends was in the middle of three sisters. Her parents were Christians and had a lovely home. I spent many nights with her enjoying their family amidst lots of laughter, fun and good food. They were a role model for me. I want my family to be a role model to others.

In the course of a conversation with my granddaughter when she was in high school, she mentioned a friend who lived with her dad. Further into the discussion she remarked about a friend who lived with her mom. I said, "Sweetie, do you have any friends who come from a home where the mother and father live together and they have a happy, loving home?"

She paused for a moment and said, "No, I don't guess I do." That broke my heart.

Marriage and families in our culture and in our churches as well, are in trouble. According to George Barna's statistics, the divorce rate in the church is now equal to that of secular society. We need to be fanatics in order to redeem our marriages and have the kind of families that honor the Lord. We can't be half-hearted in our alliance with our mates. The marriage relationship must be pursued and cultivated with care. We have to be ardent about the issue of our marriages. We must build carefully and attentively with solid bricks.

- Is your home a role model for one who may need it?

    Why or why not?

One of my favorite exercises with youth involved drawing a continuum on a white board or a chalk board, and labeling it from 1- 10. I asked the young people to put a mark on the continuum that indicated where their walk with Jesus was at the time—one being low (apathetic, disobedient, or rebellious) and ten being high (on fire for God, passionate in worship, witnessing, listening to God).

- Let's do that now:

1_____10

Most of the young people placed their marks somewhere in the middle. How did you rate your walk?

After we completed the exercise, I proceeded to read Revelation 3:15-16.

- Turn to that Scripture and read it. Why do you think the Lord prefers a believer to be hot or cold rather than lukewarm? Wouldn't it at least be better to be lukewarm than cold?

This Scripture bewildered me for a long time, until I realized that if we are hot or cold, the world around us knows where we stand—what we believe or don't believe. But when we are lukewarm, the charges of hypocrite can be hurled at us. We say one thing and live another. We don't really live what we profess.

I heard a speaker at a conference say one time, "We practice daily what we really believe. All else is religious chatter." Out of our own confession we admit to having a walk with Jesus that makes him want to vomit us out of his mouth. Why would we want to do that?

- ***Building Tool*** – When bricks are being laid in a house, they are precisely stacked one at a time, not dumped on all at once in a pile. So it is as our walk with the Lord progresses. What is one area in which you might be lukewarm, or even cold, that you would like to move closer to a ten? Be prepared to discuss this issue with your group.

We might be thinking at this point something like, "True, the Bible talks about being a fool for Christ and not being lukewarm, but this is real life. God gave you a brain to think with and figure this out for yourself. You can't go literally by everything that the Bible says."

- Do you believe we should live literally by what the Bible teaches?

    How and where do you draw the line?

Let's digress a moment to discuss briefly one of the aspects of proper Biblical interpretation, and that is determining a timeless truth from a regulation for a particular people at a particular time in history. If we fail to acknowledge this principle as we interpret Scripture we can get into a mess of legalism and rules.

A good of example of this is the issue of head coverings for women. In the book of 1 Corinthians 11:2-16 Paul discusses this topic. Some denominations still believe today that women should have their heads covered during worship—others have dispensed with the practice in recent years. How are we to apply this passage today in our culture?

In the day in which this was written, it was a disgrace for a Jewish woman to appear in public with her head uncovered. A proper Jewish woman always wore a veil, a head covering. Some devout Jewish women even kept their heads covered in the home. But the prostitutes paraded the streets shamelessly with their heads uncovered, their hair flowing and gold ornaments which sparkled in the sun beckoning customers. If a woman was found involved in adultery, her head was shaved, to her great shame. The only time a woman appeared in public with her head uncovered was when she was a bride—then she wore her hair down as she came to her bridegroom to be wed. So we see that the manner in which a woman's hair was treated spoke a message to those around her.

That is no longer true in our culture, at least to that degree. Wearing a head covering is not the timeless truth in this passage, in my opinion. I believe that the timeless truth here is submission to authority—the authority of the husband in the home and the authority of God over the husband and the couple. Paul also discusses our inter-dependence on each other, male and female, and that everything comes from God. He seems to give us the freedom to judge for ourselves. Some things seem proper in one society or culture, but not in another.

I shall never forget going on vacation with a friend and her family when I was a teenager. We lived in the Southwest, but their extended family lived in Miami, Florida. We met some Christian young people one evening who invited us to attend their church's youth activity that weekend at the beach. At the beach? Girls and boys swimming? Our conservative church at home did not allow what they called "mixed bathing" (boys and girls swimming together), but there in Miami it was the norm. The culture was a bit different, even though we all lived in the same country. What was taboo in one part of the country was actually a church activity in another.

Now back to believing the Bible literally. Yes, we are to take literally the timeless truths of the Scripture—principles such as tithing, telling the truth, no adultery, no murder and no stealing. If we try to use our human reasoning to figure out our standards of living, we begin to believe the lies of the enemy. We can't make human, logical sense out of Biblical standards such as giving in order to receive, being last instead of first, serving instead of ruling.

The Wise Woman Builds

"Yea, hath God said?" Satan's whisperings once again. The enemy caused Eve to question that God meant literally what he said. He caused her to start reasoning and rationalizing what God had instructed regarding boundaries in the Garden of Eden. He is still doing it to God's people today.

- Can you recall a time when you tried to reason out a situation logically and acted upon it only to have ended up in a mess? Write it out briefly.

- What is a literal Bible teaching that you have shied away from because you didn't want to appear to be a fanatic?

- Find it in Scripture and write out below.

The Pharisees to whom Jesus was speaking lived extremely religious lives. They performed their religious duties well. The society of their day looked to them as their spiritual leaders. Their fruit looked good. But Jesus turns and says to the crowd after all this wonderful teaching:

Not everyone who says to me, 'Lord, Lord,' will enter the kingdom of heaven, but only he who does the will of my Father who is in heaven. Many will say unto me on that day, 'Lord,

Lord, did we not prophesy in your name, and in your name drive out demons and perform many miracles?' Then I will tell them plainly, 'I never knew you. Away from me, you evildoers!' (Matthew 7:21-23).

Evildoers? They were the religious leaders of their day. They were very righteous, church-going people. This is one of the most sobering passages in all of Scripture. Jesus' teaching pierced right through all the "churchy, religious, holier-than-thou stuff."

In our common everyday language he might have sounded something like this: "Hey, I know you are at the church all the time, but what about being salt and light. Are you letting your light shine before men? Are you telling people about me? Are you honest in your business dealings with ordinary people?

"How're you doing in the area of freely forgiving your friend from the heart, guys? Don't even go to church until you do that. Simply being angry with your brother makes you subject to judgment.

"What about lustful thoughts? Oh, I know you would never stoop to actual adultery, but I saw you leering at that young lady over there. That constitutes adultery just as much as the actual act.

"What about judging your brother? Are you critical toward your brothers and sisters and fail to see your own shortcomings?

"Are you willing to go the second mile for your brother? Are you willing to love unconditionally when it is not convenient?

"You do well at loving those who are like you, but do you love your enemies—the ones who slander you and make fun of you?

"Are you giving freely to the poor, to those in need? And when you do give, do you brag about it to others, or perhaps you just subtly mention it in passing during conversation, but your friends get the point that you have given generously.

"How's your prayer life? Are you getting up each morning to spend intimate time alone with the Father—not just praying in public to be seen of men? Do you ever fast? And when you do, is it simply so others will see how righteous you are?

"Are you a worrier? Are you concerned about storing up earthly treasures—how much money you have in the your savings account, worrying about how many clothes you have in your closet, or about what you are going to eat for dinner?"

- ***Building Tool*** – This question may be difficult. Look at the list above. Ask the Lord to reveal to you where you have been substituting the letter of the law for the spirit of the law, the "churchy stuff" for the genuine item. In reality, what we are asking is, "Where have I been a hypocrite?"

We do not have time to delve individually into each of these teachings in this lesson. Each one demands study and time of its own. However, at this point, we are "gathering building materials." Are your building materials going to be bricks or sticks?

Jesus cuts away the "fluff" and gets to the heart of issues. He gets to the spirit of the law, not simply the legalistic letter of the law. The legalistic letter of the law constitutes brittle, flimsy sticks with which to build our lives. They will collapse when the storms begin to blow. The spirit of the law springs up out of the living water of a relationship with Jesus and his principles. They are the bricks that will remain strong in the hard times. Those bricks will stand firm and true. They will provide a shelter that will not disintegrate as we build our lives within its walls.

- *Building Tool* – Did you pass the hearing test? Have you gathered the proper materials with which to begin construction – bricks and not sticks? Discuss with your spouse what the Lord has revealed to you about the building materials of your home before you meet again with your ladies group.

- *Small Group Discussion*: (1) Share with the group what areas of your life and marriage are lukewarm. What elements are lacking in your building materials? They may be the same items. (2) Are you ready to gather Jesus' building materials of solid bricks and throw away the sticks, the fake stuff? Pray together with your group and ask the Lord to give you direction.

Chapter Seven

Ooops—Back To The Drawing Board!

For He knows how we are formed, He remembers that we are dust (Psalm 103:14).

We live our lives, seeking to follow the Great Architect's blueprints and plans the best we know how. Our efforts go into establishing our homes on a solid foundation—that of Jesus Christ in our marriages. We attempt to build with the solid bricks of Jesus' words, instead of with the sticks of cultural standards and mores. We are active in our church and community, but somewhere along the way, the storms come, and we find ourselves desperately propping up the walls of our flimsy houses built with sticks.

Death visits our family.

Marital difficulties crop up, even when we have sought to build a Christian marriage.

Financial problems come our way, even when we have been tithing.

Children raised right go wrong. Illness hits our household.

The company downsizes, and our spouse is laid off. A once-promising career falls flat.

We begin to doubt that Father does know best. We echo once again the question that Satan whispered in Eve's ear, "Yea, hath God said?"

But we word it differently, "Well, if God loves us so much, why did he let all this happen to us?"

Then we veer from following the blueprint on the drawing board of God's plan for our lives. Maybe we stray just a little–maybe a lot. Maybe we think, "I've been following God and look what has happened. I give up. I'm throwing in the towel. I'm going to try something else."

Or maybe we simply quit seeking the Father's guidance on a daily basis. We stop reading our Bible, quit praying and listening to his instructions. We stop following the blueprint. We basically say, "I can do a better job all by myself!"

When my brother was killed in Vietnam, it was understandably a very difficult time for our family. We had prayed diligently for my brother while he was away and believed that he would make it back home safely. He was due to process out in three weeks. We were relieved that we would see him soon. It was a crushing blow when we received the news that he would never come home again.

My mom was devastated, but she had her faith in God to cling to. She knew God was faithful even though she was heartbroken and did not understand.

Mom's faith in God was a stark contrast to my dad's lack of faith. As I sat at the funeral home with my grieving father, I once again talked to him about the Lord. His statement to me was, "I've tried that. It doesn't work."

- Perhaps you, too, have gotten to the point of saying, at least to yourself, "I've tried that. It doesn't work." To a point of not being able to trust Jesus. You have tried following Jesus and because of troubles that have come your way, you may feel as if it just doesn't work for you. What experience(s) have caused you to question God's goodness in the way he has ordered your life so far?

All of us experience failure and/or heartache in one form or another—as a wife, a mother, a friend, or a daughter. When I was a young wife and mother, I attended a Bible study on the Book of James taught by a wise seminary professor. He was addressing verse two of chapter one where James tells us: "Consider it pure joy, my brothers, whenever you face trials of many kinds…"

The professor told us that when we go through trials we are to thank God and be joyful, even in the midst of pain. He testified of several trials he had been through, and that God uses suffering to conform us to the image of Jesus.

A young woman in the back raised her hand, and in the thickest sing-song Texas accent you can imagine said, "But, sir, I've never been through anything like tha-yat. Ah've never experienced any pain lahk tha-yat."

The professor hung his head. "Oh, I wish you hadn't said that. Because you are either in a trial at the present, you have been through a trial in the past—or you *will* go through a trial in the future. If you are a true believer, trials are ahead of you. Rest assured." A holy hush fell upon the class as the lecture continued.

God's most useful servants experienced it. Abraham failed at one point to follow God's blueprint. He tried to accelerate God's plan. He couldn't see how he could possibly have a son by Sarah. Let's be practical—they were much too old. "Yea, hath God said?" There it is again.

God was taking too long. Perhaps he needed some assistance to bring his promise to Abraham to pass. Sarah took matters into her own hands and devised a plan. She would give her handmaiden, Hagar, to Abraham in an attempt to have a son. Abraham agreed, and Hagar did indeed become pregnant and had a son, Ishmael.

But Ishmael was not the son of promise, and the consequences of Abraham's not trusting the Father's blueprint for his life are still being felt in the Middle East today. Ishmael was the progenitor of the Arab nations. The prophecy spoken to Hagar concerning Ishmael is sobering in the light of escalating terrorist activities: *He will be a wild donkey of a man; his hand will be against everyone and everyone's hand against him, and he will live in hostility toward all his brothers* (Genesis 16:12). Abraham's unbelief that God would deliver what He promised resulted in repercussions still reverberating throughout the world today.

- Let's look at some Bible characters, their failures and how they responded.

Bible Character	Failure	Response
Moses (Ex. 2:11-12)		
David (2 Sam. 11)		
Job (Job 1:6-22; 2:1-10; 30-31; 42:5-6)		

Judas Iscariot (Luke 22:47-48)

Peter (John 18:15-18; 18:25-27)

- Compare and contrast Judas Iscariot's response to failure and Peter's response.

Judas Iscariot   Peter

- *Building Tool* – All of us doing this study have experienced some kind of heartache and/or failure. Pray and ask the Holy Spirit to bring to mind instances you have encountered in your journey. You may shed some tears—that's alright. Just record your experiences.

My Experiences   My Responses

Heartache and failure are unavoidable. We are sinners living in a sinful, fallen world. If we never failed, we would never know the unconditional abundance of God's grace. What we need to learn is how to allow God to use the failure and heartache for his glory. Look at the difference in the reactions of Peter and Judas Iscariot. Both denied Jesus. But Peter repented, turned and followed Jesus until the end of his life to the glory of God. Judas was sorry and went out and hung himself—but simply being sorry is not true repentance. Satan gained a victory. True repentance does not lead to destruction, but to a change of direction and restoration.

How do God's blueprints on the drawing board of our lives get messed up? And how are we to view the ruined drawings of our lives? Does God wash his hands of us? Does he punish us in kind for our failures? Are we to attempt to correct the drawing, or are we to let God do it? Should we stay away from church and other Christians until we get our act cleaned up? Let's look at Biblical attitudes toward failure and heartache, trials and suffering.

- Look up 2 Corinthians 4:7 and Psalm 103:14. What do these Scriptures say about us?

The Scriptures tell us that we are weak, frail human vessels of earth. We can thank the Lord that he remembers our frames—that we are but dust. We are going to fail. We are going to make poor choices from time to time. We are going to stumble, but God already knows that and he loves us anyway. He's not mad at us. Sometimes we can find Him more real in our stumbling, if we respond correctly and repent and lay the broken pieces of our lives at his feet to mend, repair to be useful again.

- Turn to John 8 and read verses 1-11.

Down through the ages, the account of the woman taken in adultery has spoken particularly to women of the inherent compassion and mercy of our Lord Jesus.

Put yourself in the picture portrayed in the Scriptures. Jesus arrives at the Temple early in the morning with His disciples. The dawn is breaking over the eastern horizon painting the Jerusalem sky with florescent pinks and oranges. We join a group of people gathering around, preparing to sit at the Master's feet and listen to him expound on the Scriptures.

A group of Pharisees and teachers of the law approaching amidst shouts and scuffling feet interrupt the quiet. The robes they wear identify them. They are pulling and dragging a woman toward Jesus. Her clothes have been torn from her. She is desperately grasping at the remnants of her robe to cover her nakedness.

The religious mob tosses the woman like a rag doll in front of Jesus. "Teacher, this woman was caught in the act of adultery. In the law Moses commanded us to stone such women. Now. What do *you* say?"

"Where is her partner, if she was caught in the very act?" someone whispers. "The law requires both to be brought before the priest."

Instead Jesus bends down and starts to write on the ground with his finger. What is he doing? And then we remember that curious law in the Book of Numbers, the Law of the Jealous Husband. A woman suspected of adultery could to be brought before a priest at the Temple by her husband. To determine guilt or innocence, the priest would scoop up dust from the Temple floor, make a concoction of bitter herbs and water and give it to her to drink. If her stomach bloated, she was guilty and was to be stoned. If her stomach did not bloat, she was innocent and free to go. That must be what Jesus is doing. He is going to scoop up dust for the woman to drink to judge her guilt or innocence. She is trembling and cowering before the crowd.

Jesus stands up and begins to speak to the men, their faces red with rage. Quietly, but firmly, Jesus says, "If any one of you is without sin, let him be the first to throw a stone at her." He stoops down again, but he is not scooping up dust. He is writing in the sand.

The crowd begins to disperse—the older ones leaving first, dropping their stones, impotent in the dust. We hear Jesus speaking to the woman, as we turn, embarrassed, and leave with the others, "Woman where are they? Has no one condemned you?"

We hear her soft reply, "No one, sir."

"Then neither do I condemn you. Go now and leave your life of sin."

- With whom, in that passage, do you most identify? The woman? The bystanders?

  The religious crowd – ready to throw stones? Cite reasons for the answer you give.

- Do you think this woman had strayed from the blueprint God had for her?

  Why or why not?

- Can she still be effective in the Kingdom of God?

  Why or why not?

- Had the Pharisees strayed from God's blueprint?

  How?

- Can they still be effective in the Kingdom of God?

- Have you strayed from the blueprint God has for you?

  How?

- Can you still be effective in the Kingdom of God?

  Why or why not?

- Reread one of our earlier memory verses, Psalm 145:8-9,14.

Another reason for stumbling—and one that we often overlook—is the fact that a spiritual battle is raging around us and most of us go on about our lives blissfully unaware of that fact. Then when we stumble and fall, or some startling news comes our way, we are totally shocked. We walked into the enemy's territory in the middle of a battle that day without putting on our armor, and then we are surprised when we get wounded. Or we don't even show up for the battle.

Peter told us, "Hey, guys, don't be shocked when you go through fiery trials. That's not so strange." (My paraphrase from I Peter 4:12.)

We shouldn't be surprised when the fiery darts of Satan come our way. The blueprint of our lives sometimes gets marred because we are the target of the enemy. I Peter 5:8 tells us, "Your enemy the devil prowls around like a roaring lion looking for someone to devour." We are being stalked!

- Read John 10:10. What is the mission of the enemy?

- Are you shocked when crises come in your life?
  Why or why not?

Satan's mission is to steal, kill and destroy, but through Jesus we can ultimately be victorious over the enemy as we trust the Lord and press on through trials.

- What does Romans 8:37 tell us?

- Read 2 Cor. 10:3-6. What weapons do we have?

But, we must show up prepared for battle, even if we had rather not. Every Christian is a target of our enemy. Victory is already ours, but we must put on our armor and face the enemy. We cannot retreat.

- Read Ephesians 6:10-17. A word is repeated three times in that passage which tells us we cannot turn and run, we must:

- Ephesians 6:10-17 also names the pieces of armor that we are to wear. List them below; designate what is represented by each piece of the armor; and how you can apply each representation to your life.

Piece of Armor   Represents   Application

*Note to leader: If you are the leader of this Bible study, you may want to do some additional study on the armor of God.

- What does verse 18 say we are to do after putting on the armor of God?

- What does that tell you about the battleground?

- Where, then, would you say a wise woman would find directions to follow the blueprint in order to build her home?

- ***Building Tool*** – In your prayer time this week, practice putting on the armor of God. Record below what insights God gives you as you stand and pray.

I don't relish the thought, but God uses trials and suffering to teach and discipline us as a father. We don't mature in a context of ease. An old saying goes something like this, "Calm seas do not skilled sailors make."

We grow up in the context of struggle. We mature even when we have been offended by the Lord—when we rage and shake our fist at God and shout, "You are not fair, God! You are unjust—where are you?" If we will press through that experience clinging to the Lord, our walk with Him will develop strong faith muscles.

- Have you ever been offended by God? Be brutally honest. Describe the incident(s) and what feelings you experienced.

- Find a Scriptural example of someone who was offended by God. (E.g. Job)

When trials and suffering come our way to discipline us, we have a choice.

- Look at Hebrews 12:3-13 and see if you can find four ways to deal with discipline.

    (1)

    (2)

    (3)

    (4)

    (1) Verse 5 tells us we can "blow it off" ("take lightly") or (2) cry, moan and complain, faint and lose heart or (3) we can grit our teeth and endure it like a martyr - verse 7; or we can (4) accept the discipline and live - verse 9.

- Which verse describes how you deal with discipline?

    Write it below.

I've noticed that most of us, who are followers of Jesus, do well when the big, traumatic events come our way. However, it seems that getting outside the lines of the blueprint comes in the little, insignificant, daily "busyanity" of our lives. That is where we stumble. But that is where faithfulness in walking through trials truly produces fruit. That is discipline—to carry out the insignificant practices of daily routine—to go to work, to make the bed every morning, to prepare daily meals, to pray daily, to scrub the kitchen floor, to take out the trash, to perform excellently on our job, to care for a disabled child or invalid parent. It is in those daily disciplines that we are building homes, forging destinies and producing good fruit.

- ***Small Group Discussion***: (1) Share with your group a time of heartache, failure or trials that caused you to question the Father's plans for your life. (2) What was your primary struggle? Maintaining an attitude of gratitude? (3) Are you willing to get back on the drawing board and let the Architect finish? Close with prayer making that commitment.

Chapter Eight

Wormwood and Gall

Be kind and compassionate to one another, forgiving each other, just as in Christ God forgave

you (Ephesians 4:32).

After dealing with discipline in Hebrews 12, the writer warns us in verse 15 against letting bitterness take root.

- Read that verse in two or three different versions. What leads to bitterness?

If we are not careful, when we go through difficult times, whether it is our own failures and stumblings, warfare or discipline, we can become bitter. If we do not submit to the discipline and training of the Lord, our hearts become hard and bitterness can set in. Notice that when we become bitter, it doesn't just affect ourselves personally. Many become contaminated and defiled by it—our families, our friends, our brothers and sisters in Christ.

- Read 1 Thessalonians 5:18. How do we avoid the pitfall of bitterness?

First, we are to give thanks *in* all things. Note that it does not say *for* all things, but *in* all things. An attitude of gratitude will go a long way to preventing bitterness. There is hardly anyone less pleasant to be around than a bitter, hardened, pessimistic person—one who always views the glass as half empty. And no one is more enjoyable to have in your company than a cheerful, grateful, optimistic saint, who views the glass half-full.

- Name a circumstance in the midst of which it was difficult for you to give thanks.

- Turn to Ephesians 4:32. What is another way to avoid bitterness?

We could spend this entire study talking about forgiveness, but basically, we are to freely forgive, as he has forgiven us. How can we hold a grudge when we think of Jesus giving up his life on the cross to pay for our sins?

"But you don't know what they did to me!" you may say. No, I don't, but I know what they did to Jesus, and he forgave. We have no justification to hold anything against a brother or sister in light of the cross. He is the only one who has a right to be bitter and unforgiving—and he isn't.

We must let all bitterness go. The Amplified Bible says:

Let all bitterness and indignation and wrath, passion, rage, bad temper, and resentment, anger, animosity, and quarreling, brawling, clamor, contention, and slander, evil speaking, abusive or blasphemous language be banished from you, with all malice, spite, ill will or baseness of any kind. And become useful and helpful and kind to one another, tenderhearted, forgiving one another readily and freely, as God in Christ forgave you (Ephesians 4:31-32).

That's a tall order, isn't it? But very clear. We are to forgive one another as Jesus forgives us and not allow ourselves to become bitter.

The Greek word in the New Testament for forgiveness is *aphiaymi*, which means to abandon, let go, send away. To forgive another does not mean we have to emotionally feel forgiving. It does mean we must let go of the issue and let God deal with it. It means we lay aside any slander or review of the offense or the offender. We refuse to nurse it, curse it, or rehearse it, but we give it to God to reverse it and disburse it.

- Let's administer a quick test to see whether there is any bitterness or unforgiveness lurking in your heart. Do you feel anyone owes you anything?

Write down any names that might come across your mind.

Is there anything in the midst of which you have not been able to give thanks?

Have you been guilty of nursing, cursing or rehearsing a wrong done to you?

Are you willing to give it to God to reverse and disburse it?

We must be quick to forgive. Forgiveness is canceling the debt and bringing the balance to zero. The offender owes you nothing. We are called to give a blessing, not an insult. God is at work and He knows what He is doing with our lives. We must not struggle against the process.

- *Building Tool* - If you answered in the affirmative to the quick test above, you may be harboring unforgiveness toward someone. If the Holy Spirit has brought someone to mind, you may need to make a phone call or write a note asking for his/her forgiveness. Just a short note or conversation will do. Something like, "God has convicted me that I was wrong in _____. Would you please forgive me?" You don't need to go into all the details. The other person may try to recount the details of the offense, or you may become defensive. Just let it go. Simply repeat, "It would mean an awful lot to me, if you would forgive me. Would you please forgive me?" Be prepared to share with your group.

Not long ago I had to call my oldest and closest friend from childhood and ask her to forgive me for a judgmental attitude towards her. I truly had not meant to be judgmental, but she felt I was judging her, so I called and asked her forgiveness.

My first reaction, when she said, "You were being judgmental," was to defend myself. But the Lord stopped me, and I simply asked her again to forgive me. She did, and our relationship was restored. Tension hung in the air when I talked to her or saw her before I made the phone call. Now it is like old times. Now we are free in our relationship once again.

You may think of an instance where you feel completely justified. I find it easy to rationalize my own behavior. We will *always* feel justified. Let's say I am one per cent wrong and the other party is ninety-nine per cent wrong. God still requires me to take care of my one per cent. It may simply be that the attitude has been wrong, but I won't be free of it until I forgive and ask for forgiveness.

When I speak at women's retreats and conferences across the country, I consistently have occasion to deal with this issue of bitterness and unforgiveness. One young woman at a retreat, divorced and bitter, declared that she didn't care who told her she had to forgive, she was *never* going to forgive her ex-spouse. As far as I know, she left the retreat in that condition. It grieved me, and I know it grieved the heart of God as well.

The issue is not between the offender and us. The issue is between God and us. Are we going to be obedient to what his word instructs us to do? Or are we going to be rebellious and refuse to follow the blueprint that he has set down for our own good?

The problem won't go away automatically as if by magic by itself. The offense will play like videotape in our minds until we deal with it. Forgiveness is a choice. I choose to let it go and let God handle the other person. I am convinced that something happens in the supernatural when we choose to forgive. That is when the healing begins.

Forgiveness does not mean forgetting. God does not expect us to suddenly develop spiritual amnesia. It means we remember the offense against the offender no more. We do not hold it against them. Memory serves as a catalyst to godly behavior the next time a similar situation arises. We are not called on to erase a memory.

Forgiveness does not mean allowing yourself to be in harm's way. In abusive situations, the proper action and indeed, the spiritual and Christian thing to do, is to remove yourself and your children. Too many times my husband and I have counseled with women in an abusive situation who have been taught a warped interpretation of submission. They have been told that staying with an abusive spouse is the Biblical choice to make. We have found that most of the time a separation will catapult the husband into the counseling help that he needs, whereas if the wife and children remain in the home, he never seeks the proper counsel.

However, removing oneself from the home does not release one from the responsibility of forgiving. I spoke to a recently divorced woman at a conference whose husband had been violently abusive. In fact, he had been extradited to another state. When I explained that she must forgive him, her eyes widened in surprise. But as she began to understand that forgiveness did not condone his behavior, but released him to God, she was able to pray and forgive him. That did not mean that there would be no consequences, punishment or discipline. It did mean that she was taking her former husband off her "hit list," so to speak, and putting him on God's "hit list.'

I have a pastor friend who prays for his enemies like so, "God, get them." Any manner in which God "gets them" is going to be for their good—whether by salvation or through chastisement.

Even when it seems the blueprint is such a mess that it cannot be fixed, God can redo the drawing so that it works together for good. Even our stumblings, our heartaches, our hardships and trials can be used for his glory. The problem is that we have the choice of climbing off the drawing board. Let's determine to remain on the drawing board no matter how painful until the Great Architect has finished his adjustments and corrections to the plans.

- ***Small Group Discussion***: (1) Have you allowed yourself to become bitter over a situation? Have you had a struggle with forgiveness? Share your struggle with your group and ask them to pray with you. (2) Did the Lord prompt you to ask forgiveness for an offense this week? Share it with your group. Use discretion. You don't need to mention names.

Chapter Nine

Decorating The House

And by knowledge shall the chambers (of its every area) be filled with all precious and pleasant

riches" (Proverbs 24:4 Amp).

Our house is set solidly on the foundation of Jesus Christ. The walls are fortified with the bricks of the words of Jesus. We have encountered heartache and difficulties along the way. We may have strayed from the blueprint a bit and tried to draw our own plans, but we got back on track, and our house is sturdy. The next question is: How are we going to fill the rooms and decorate the house?

The Scripture says, "…by knowledge shall the chambers be filled…" That is a nice verse, but what does it mean? It's one of those verses we kind of flit by and never land on. What kind of knowledge—and filled with what? What do the terms "precious and pleasant riches" mean?

Let's look first at "knowledge." The Hebrew word for knowledge comes from the root word, *yada,* meaning "to know." *Yada* has a variety of meanings, including recognition, observation, discernment, and instruction. One of its primary meanings as used in Scripture is "intimate knowledge." It is the word used for intimate relations between a man and a woman. Genesis 4:1 says in the King James, "And Adam *knew* Eve his wife; and she conceived, and bare Cain..." (emphasis mine). Intimate knowledge.

- Look up Psalm 46:10a. Write it out.

- If you have a Strong's concordance, look up the word "know" as used in this passage. What is the Hebrew word here for "know?"

- Read Proverbs 3:5-6. Look up the word "acknowledge" in your Strong's concordance. What is the Hebrew word?

Yada is the kind of union God desires with us as His children. He wants us to have an intimate relationship with him as our Father.

- Look up Psalm 46:10a. What does this verse seem to say we need to do in order to get to "know" God?

- When we love someone, we will sacrifice to get to know them intimately. Why is "being still" such a sacrifice for us?

When Adam had intimate relations with Eve, fruit resulted. She had a son. When we seek to know God intimately, fruit will result.

- Galatians 5:22-23 enumerates the fruit of the Spirit. List them here:

- Do you suppose that when we have intimate fellowship with the Father that the fruit of the Spirit would be evident in our lives?

  Why?

- Read John 15:1-8. How do we bear fruit?

Jesus tells us in this passage that if we are abiding in him, that we will bear fruit. I heard someone say one time that we are simply racks to hang fruit upon. We don't have to stress and strain and worry about proper food, or water, or cultivation. Our Father is the gardener. He will attend to all that. All we have to do is intimately abide in Jesus.

I am concerned that many of us feel this type of intimate relationship with the Father is only for the so-called "stars" in Christendom, i.e. Madame Guyon, St. Augustine, Martin Luther, C. S. Lewis, Mother Teresa, Billy Graham.

A neighbor of ours had cancer several years ago. We received the news recently that the cancer had returned, and she would be undergoing chemotherapy and radiation treatment once again. I called to assure her we would be praying for her. Her response was "Oh, thank you, so much. I know your prayers reach heaven quicker than mine."

Somehow, we have the idea that just because someone is a pastor, or an evangelist or a Christian leader of some kind, that they have a "hot line" to heaven. We all, as believers, have that "hot line" to heaven. All those who desire to walk closer to the Lord have the opportunity to develop intimate fellowship with the Father.

- Turn to Matthew 5:6 and read it. What is the requirement for being filled up?

- Read Psalm 42:1. Describe in your own words how a deer reacts when thirsty.

- Are you desperately thirsty for God and His righteousness?

Have you ever seen livestock head for a water hole? They plunge headlong with their entire focus on that water. Nothing stands in their way. And they don't stop until they have their fill of water and slake their thirst.

I wonder, "Do I have that kind of longing to know the Lord more—the kind of desperation we experience when we are really thirsty?"

I don't believe I have ever really been thirsty more than a few hours. However, I have seen firsthand how dangerous dehydration can be and how quickly it can occur. When our oldest grandson, Cody, was three years old he contracted a stomach virus. Our daughter and her family were living in a small town across the state from us. She had just given birth to her third child in four years, and my husband and I had gone out to visit the new addition and help out for a few days. Understandably, she was distracted with the newborn baby and her many duties at home. Cody became dehydrated, almost without any of us noticing it, but my husband became alarmed and took him to the hospital.

We nearly lost Cody that night. The medical staff could hardly find a vein into which they could insert the IV because of the dehydration. He did recover and after a few days was able to go back home to the family. Going without fluids is dangerous for our physical bodies.

Going without living water is dangerous for our spiritual bodies. Drinking from the living water satisfies and brings us into intimate fellowship with God. If we allow our spirits to become dehydrated, we are in danger of something within us withering away, just as Cody's veins deflated because of the lack of moisture.

It troubles me that we, who are leaders in churches, have been so focused on bringing people into the Kingdom that perhaps we have not taught our people how to develop a deep relationship with Jesus for themselves—how to fill their homes with the intimate knowledge of God. We have allowed our flocks to settle for wading in stagnant streams of mere church attendance week after week instead of leading them to drink deeply for themselves from the living water, which Jesus promises to give us if we come to Him (John 4:10).

When we thirst desperately after God, it produces the kind of knowledge that will fill up our homes with beautiful furnishings. Let's look at some of the practicalities of *yada* with the Father.

We discussed in an earlier lesson about a daily quiet time with God. I imagine by this time you are on your way to forming that habit. Hopefully, those times with the Lord are becoming more and more precious. I pray you are hearing him speak to you through the Word. I trust you are beginning to be able to hear the "word within the Word"—that special insight with which God convicts you and penetrates your heart that perhaps nobody else sees.

- Are you meeting with Jesus everyday? Write down some insights He has been giving you—the "word within the Word."

As we continue to consider this concept of *yada,* I would like to discuss at this point a deeper, more intimate communication with the Father in our prayer lives. I want you to know as we study this topic that I am a fellow struggler right along with you. I know of no other aspect in the Christian journey that is more difficult for all of us than this mystery of prayer. We will learn together.

- Turn to Matthew 6:9-13 and read through the model prayer.

- Focus on verse 9. To whom is the prayer addressed?

When we go to the Lord in prayer, we are going as a child to her Father. Please note that an intimate relationship is already assumed. We are coming to Abba Father—"Daddy." We are his daughters. However, it may be difficult for some of us to relate to a loving heavenly Father.

I did not enjoy the privilege of having a loving, earthly father. My dad was from a large family of eight children. His father was the owner and editor of five newspapers. The family considered themselves intellectuals of sorts, although none of them, as far I know, were formally educated. All of the men in the family were writers and authors and newspapermen as well. But it was not a happy family. Alcoholism ran its steely fingers through the lineage holding several of the siblings captive in its vice. There was never any outward demonstration of affection, hugging or embracing that I remember. The only laughter came from reactions to dry wit and cutting humor due to their language skills honed razor sharp as a result of their occupation.

I never remember having a decent conversation with my dad. The only time he spoke to me was to scold me for some offense. He worked at night frequently, and waking him up for any reason was strictly taboo. I remember no hugs from him as a child, or telling me that he loved me, or that I was pretty, or that he was proud of me. You can readily see, therefore, because of the example of my earthly father, why I might have had difficulty relating to my heavenly Father as one who loves me lavishly, wants to spend time with me, and desires the best for me.

- Relate your relationship with your earthly father. Has it helped or hindered in being intimate in your relationship with your heavenly Father?

- If you had a kind, loving earthly father, stop right now and write out a prayer below, thanking God for him.

- If you did not have a loving earthly father, thank God that he is a loving heavenly Father who cares deeply for you. Feel his arms around you as you pray.

- *Building Tool* – If your earthly father is still living, and he was a good model for you, write him a note expressing your love and gratitude to him. Perhaps he wasn't perfect—who is? Pick out the traits that you admire in him and tell him. Perhaps your earthly father is no longer living. Write out a letter to him anyway expressing your feelings and debt of gratitude to him.

- If your earthly father was not a good model and is still living, is there anything you can do to try to mend the relationship? Ask forgiveness for your attitude toward him? Talk to him about his relationship to the Lord? Pray diligently for him? Write down what action you need to take.

- Be prepared to discuss the relationship you have or had with your earthly father, whether good or bad, with your group.

After addressing the Father in the model prayer, Jesus praises him and declares him as holy, "Hallowed be Thy name." Praise and adoration rightly should be first on our agenda of prayer. I will admit that is difficult for me. I am not flowery of speech. I am a "bottom-line" type person. What has helped me greatly at this point is to turn in my Bible to one of the Psalms written about the Lord's majesty and glory, or his mercy and loving-kindness and read it as an expression of praise and adoration—Psalms such as 103 which we will read below. I have heard some start their prayers with a ritualistic heading, "Lord, we come to you with praise and adoration…" There's nothing wrong with that, but I don't think that is exactly what Jesus had in mind. I believe he would like us to take some time and meditate on his goodness to us and upon the majesty of his creation. I believe he wants us to reflect on the awesomeness of his character.

- Turn to Psalm 103 and read it silently. Now read it out loud. What did the Lord do in your spirit as you read the Psalm out loud?

Praying Scripture has been probably the greatest asset to strengthening my prayer life in the area of praise and adoration. I do not honestly remember where or from whom I learned about this concept, but I can think of no other one thing that has been as beneficial to me. Praying Scripture deepens and quickens the intimate relationship we have with our heavenly Father. It intensifies the *yada* we enjoy with the Lord. Intimacy with God is spirit to spirit. That is why reading and quoting Scripture back to him plumbs the depths of our soul, and we make contact.

Not only do reading and quoting Scriptures help us touch the heart of God in prayer, the Holy Spirit comes to our rescue as well.

- Read Romans 8:26-27. What is that verse saying to you?

When we don't know what to pray, the Scripture tells us the Holy Spirit will pray for us. He will bring people and situations to our hearts for which to pray. He will articulate to God the

Father the inner longings of our hearts that we are unable to verbalize.

Understandably, our children, grandchildren and families are uppermost on our hearts as we come to the Lord in prayer. Through the years the Holy Spirit has quickened my spirit to specific Scriptures as I agonized in prayer over my children or a particular situation. Our oldest daughter and I were driving back from a trip after she had been married several years and had five children. We began talking about how I had prayed Scripture for her through the years. I commenced to read the Scriptures I had prayed for her and the dates written down beside the passages. She was amazed at how God had answered in such specific ways.

- Read Colossians 1:9-14. This is a passage that I have prayed over our family for years. Has the Lord ever given you a passage to pray over your family? Write it out.

- *Building Tool* -- If praying Scripture is new to you, perhaps you would like to pray the Colossians passage over your family as well. Read it aloud several times and get it into your heart and spirit. Or perhaps you would like to choose another Scripture. Pick a passage out and share it with your spouse. Ask him if he would agree to pray the passage for your family along with you. If you are a single mom, the responsibility lies with you. Choose a passage and begin praying it over your children.

As we pray in this manner, we are in effect asking for the kingdom of God to be made manifest in the lives of our families. We are decorating the rooms with the fruit of *yada* with the Father – with love and joy and peace, kindness, goodness, faithfulness, gentleness and self-control. Just as we notice beautifully appointed furnishings in a friend's homes when we visit, these attributes will be evident to those who enter our homes.

We cannot trust our flesh to determine the object of our prayers. If we do that, our prayers become entirely self-centered. I am grateful God did not answer some of my selfish prayers in years past. The Scripture we are going to look at next is a sobering one.

- Read Psalm 106:15. Did God answer prayer here?

  What happened?

God gave the children of Israel their desires, but sent "leanness into their soul" as the Amplified translates it. The more we incorporate Scripture into our prayers, the more we see God's heart and know that for which *he* wants us to pray.

God knows that we have human concerns on our hearts as we come to him in prayer. Psalm 37:4 reads, "…He (God) will give you the desires of your heart." Jesus said in Luke 11:9, "Ask and it will be given to you." James 4:2 says, "You do not have, because you do not ask."

- Do the above Scriptures mean that God will give us every desire and whim of our hearts?

- Read those verses again in context: Psalm 37:4-5, Luke 11:9-13, and James 4:1-3. In the context of the surrounding verses, what conditions are required in order to receive that for which we ask?

  Promise   Condition

Psalm 37:4-5

Luke 11:9-13

James 4:1-3

- Cite an example when you prayed for a desire and how God answered.

When we have intimate fellowship with the Father, we will develop a trust level that he knows what is best for us and will not give us anything that will be detrimental to us. At the same time, the desires of our hearts are being turned to what he wants for us.

It is most delightful to an earthly parent to observe a child's aspirations to please. I noticed a high trust level in our daughters toward their daddy as they were growing up. I even watched one of our girls jump from the rooftop of our house into her daddy's arms when she was a pre-teen. That was because she knew she could trust the strong arms of her daddy to catch her and keep her safe.

Our daughters also learned what pleased their daddy. They knew what they could ask for. They knew anything that was not for their good, or was detrimental to them, was not allowed. The majority of the time, they trusted their daddy's judgment. On those occasions they decided to step outside of what their daddy desired for them, they got burned. Sometimes slightly, sometimes severely, depending on how far outside the line they stepped.

- Cite an example of when you asked for something amiss.

Sometimes daddies have to say "no." That is an answer as well as responding in the affirmative.

• How did God answer your prayer when you prayed amiss?

• Did you get "burned?"

How?

The passage in Luke describes an aspect of coming to know the Father that is difficult for us to understand, and that is the persistence of prayer. The Amplified says it this way, "Ask and keep on asking, and it shall be given you; seek and keep on seeking, and you shall find; knock and keep on knocking, and the door shall be opened to you."

If we want to fill our homes with *yada* knowledge of the Father, we have to be persistent. Once we have discerned God's will in a matter, we must persevere until God answers. It may be years before we see the outcome.

When our middle daughter and her family moved into their new home, she was anxious to get the 3,000 square foot house completely decorated all at once. "Sweetie," I said, "it takes years to decorate a home." It takes no time at all to put the essentials into each room—beds, couches, a table and chairs—but the finishing touches take the refining of living in the rooms to give them the polished patina of the passing seasons. Meaningful pictures will be hung. A sentimental memento picked up on a trip can be exhibited on the shelf on a bookcase and children's school projects displayed.

• Is there something for which you have been praying for a long time, but have not seen it come to pass? What is it?

- Are you praying in the Father's will?

If so, be encouraged and persevere. In the Father's time, it will come to pass and you can decorate your home with it.

- ***Building Tool*** – Discuss with your spouse or your group a prayer you have been bringing to the Lord for a long time. Ask them to pray with you. Pray afresh and anew expecting God's answer in his time. Write your prayer of praise to him that you trust him and are waiting expectantly for his answer.

Let's talk for the remainder of this lesson about the "pleasant and precious riches" the Proverbs passage mentions. We are seeking *yada* knowledge, that intimate fellowship with the Father, which fills up the rooms of our houses with these pleasant and precious riches.

The Hebrew word here for "riches" is *hown.* It means "wealth" and is used in the sense of "enough." What encouragement! I have never seen a teaching on this anywhere else. I believe the depth of this Scripture has been overlooked. In my opinion, the writer is telling us that when we seek wisdom, the Lord gives us riches that are enough to meet whatever needs we might have. God is faithful to meet our needs when we are truly seeking to follow after him.

We were going through a difficult financial struggle at one point. We found ourselves after payday without enough money to pay both the tithe and our electric bill. I held up the electric bill in one hand and our tithe check in the other. "The utility company or the tithe?" I asked my husband.

We struggled briefly with the decision as to what we should do, but knew in our hearts that we must be faithful with the tithe. God would take care of us. Going back to the definition of wisdom, which we coined in the first chapter, *comprehensive insight into the ways and purposes of God*, we decided to do it God's way and not man's way. I worked in the office at our church, so I took the tithe check into work that morning and gave it to the bookkeeper.

Later that afternoon I came back to my desk after break and found a blank envelope lying on my desk. The associate pastor walked by with a twinkle in his eye and said, "Don't ask any questions."

I opened the envelope to find $1000 check from the church. I had not shared our dilemma with anyone. I don't know to this day who gave the money. I simply bowed my head and said "Thank you, Lord."

As I left the church building after an aerobics class that same afternoon, a huge box of groceries awaited me in the hallway. I had to call my husband to come help me get the box to the car. There was an abundance of God's provision for us because we had responded in God's way to a crisis.

- Perhaps you have a similar story of God's abundance when you thought the situation was hopeless. Write it out below.

- "Bow your head and say thank you." Write out a prayer of praise and thanksgiving to

God for his provision to you.

So, we see that because we are seeking to know God intimately he is furnishing and filling up our rooms with "enough."

- Read the Scriptures listed below. What do these passages say to you about "enough?"

<u>Scripture</u>

Psalm 37:25:

Malachi 3:10:

Matthew 6:8:

Matthew 14:20:

God is filling our rooms with "enough" and not only is there an abundance of what we need, it is pleasant and precious. The word translated "pleasant" is *na'iym*. One of the meanings of the root word is "to be agreeable." The atmosphere in a Christian home should be overflowing with love, acceptance and forgiveness. Because my home was filled with tension when I was growing up, I found solace in other arenas—school, piano, friends' homes and families. When there is tension and strife in a home, for whatever reason, it is evident almost from the moment one walks in the door. I have been in Christian homes where dissension permeated every corner of the house. That should not be. Obviously the Prince of Peace is not reigning in the home where this is the case. Our homes should be havens of safety and security for our families. Children should feel free to approach their parents with any subject they need to discuss and know they are still loved and accepted.

Keeping the atmosphere clear in a home sometimes requires parents to " 'fess up" when we have blown it. What parent hasn't displayed uncalled-for anger at a child at one time or another? What parent hasn't suspected a child of some misdeed when the child was completely innocent? Just as we require our children to repent and ask forgiveness when they are wrong, we parents need to reciprocate with our children when we are wrong. We should be willing to do whatever is necessary to make our homes "agreeable."

When our youngest daughter was a freshman in college, I made a harsh comment about one of her new friends, out of concern for her. It crushed her. She left our house upset. I quickly recognized my failure. I found a suitable card, wrote a short note asking her to forgive me, and mailed it that next week. She readily forgave me, and our relationship was restored. We must move quickly toward forgiveness—especially within our immediate family. Do whatever is necessary to maintain the atmosphere of love, acceptance, and forgiveness in your home.

- *Building Tool* – Discuss with your mate whether there are any points of tension in your home. What can you do to remedy the situation? Do your children feel safe and secure in your home? Is there anything for which either of you needs to ask forgiveness from the children? Pray together and ask the Lord to show you.

Following the Lord's instructions as we furnish with *yada* knowledge of him, our homes will be filled to overflowing with precious and pleasant riches.

- ***Small Group Discussion***: (1) Discuss your relationship with your earthly father, whether it was positive or negative, and how it has affected your relationship with your heavenly Father. (2) Share with your group the Scripture passages you chose to pray over your family. Give reasons why you chose those particular Scriptures. (3) Share with your group a prayer you have been praying for a long time. Ask them to begin to pray with you about the issue. (4) Do you have a testimony about God's provision? Share it with your group. Do you have a need? Share that as well and pray expectantly for God to provide.

Chapter Ten

Occupying The House

"But in a great house there are not only vessels of gold and of silver, but also of wood and of earth; and some to honour, and some to dishonour" (2 Timothy 2:20 KJV).

Old homes are one of my favorite places to visit when we are on vacation. We have toured everything from plantations in the old South to castles in England and Ireland to a first century home in Israel. I am fascinated, not only because they have withstood the ravages of the storms of time due to their firm foundations and quality of the materials used in the building, but also because of the history contained within the walls. I try to imagine the lives of the occupants. I look at the dishes and the utensils and picture the families who sat around the dining room tables and laughed and cried together.

Antique stores and galleries also are frequent haunts of ours when we travel. Just this week we visited a huge antique mall, which had at one time been a movie theatre. I wandered up and down rows and rows of curios garnered from times gone by.

I am always on the lookout for blue and white dishes of any pattern and cobalt blue glasses and containers. My eyes are quick to spot them. Some of the vessels are valuable, like "Flow Blue"—old pottery or china on which the blue dye ran and faded when it was formed. The fault of the past on these pieces has developed into a soft, iridescent blue glow that is charming and is much in demand. They are usually expensive and displayed in cases under lock and key.

Some articles in antique stores are not as costly and are exhibited on tabletops. Others, perhaps cracked or damaged in some manner, are simply thrown in a box to gather dust.

- Look up Isaiah 29:16, Isaiah 45:9, Jeremiah 18:2-6 and Romans 9:21. What do these passages tell us about the potter?

- What do you think a vessel of honor or a vessel for noble purposes might be?

- What might a vessel of dishonor or ignoble purposes be?

When I think of a vessel of honor, I think of the silver goblets that I inherited from my mother-in-law. They are elegantly simple. I use them very seldom, and then usually for flowers.

Our middle daughter and her husband used them from which to take communion at their wedding. Or I think of the silver casserole holder that we received as a wedding present. When I want to set a refined and exquisite table, I pull the silver goblets and the silver casserole holder out of the china cabinet.

On the other hand, if I want to cook a pot of beans, make cornbread and have iced tea, I would never consider using the silver casserole container and the silver goblets. I think of my iron kettle and iron skillet and my heavy iced tea tumblers. They are not nearly as pretty, but they are practical and get the job done.

Then there are containers that I use for trash and garbage and compost that I hide away, not for public view. They are not for display.

- Think of some "vessels of honor" in your china cabinet or kitchen cabinets at home. List them and tell why they are "vessels of honor" (e.g. wedding gifts or items inherited from family).

- List some of your more "common vessels."

Of course, Paul is not talking here about literal pots and pans and silver goblets. He is making a comparison to the believer and what kind of vessel we are for the Lord.

- Which kind of "vessel" do you feel you are in the house, one of honor or a common vessel? Give reasons why.

"Now wait a minute!" you might say. "Why is one person a vessel of honor, and I feel like a common vessel? Why didn't God choose me to be a vessel of honor, too? That's not fair!"

My husband used to tell our girls, "God is not fair—he is just."

Or you may say, "I don't want to be a vessel of honor. I just want to be common."

God chooses how he will use us. We cannot control to what mission God calls us. All we can do is be obedient to occupy the house in the manner in which he called us.

- Turn to the Isaiah 45:9 passage again and using it as a guide, write out a monologue that might occur between your "vessels of honor" and your "common vessels."

- Turn to Jeremiah 18:2-6 and read verse 6 carefully. Can God not do with us as he pleases? What are your feelings reading this passage? Does it stir up resentment, or are you comforted by it?

  Explain your feelings.

God calls some of us to be "up front" in ministry. These are the preachers and teachers and evangelists, the singers and musicians, the speakers who lead conferences. They are put on display in the house. God has gifted them with talents and spiritual gifts, which lend themselves to these types of ministry.

Some giftings are very practical, and those persons with those gifts render absolutely necessary tasks, but they work in the background. They perform tasks such as janitoring, setting up of chairs, repairing the electrical and plumbing systems, serving in the kitchen. Some people are called to work with the poor, the downtrodden, those in society who have been tossed aside.

- Read through the lists of spiritual gifts found in Romans 12:3-8, 1 Corinthians 12:4-11 and Ephesians 4:11-13. What is the common thread running through all three of these lists?

- List all the gifts you find in these Scriptures.

The gifts are given sovereignly by God—differing gifts to various members of the Body, for the common good of the Body. Every believer has been given at least one gift to be used in the ministry of the church. Some have more than one gift, but every member has at least one. We have no choice in the matter. It is not a supermarket, where we go up and down the aisles and choose what looks good to us. "Oh, I would like one of those. And I think I'll have some of that, as well."

When we accept Jesus as our Redeemer, Lord and Savior, the Holy Spirit comes bearing gifts. God gifts and calls us according to his sovereign will.

- Perhaps you have done much study in the past on the spiritual gifts and know them well. Or perhaps you have never been exposed to them at all. Below I have listed definitions for the spiritual gifts you found in the Scriptures. Whether you are an old "pro" or a novice, try to match the definitions with the gifts. The answers are at the end, but don't peek until you have tried matching them on your own.

___Prophecy

a. Communicating the gospel with power and persuasiveness.

___Service

b. The ability to open new areas of work, such as missionaries, with church planting in mind, and act as a "father" to the new work.

___Teaching

c. Drawing alongside to comfort, encourage, rebuke and give insight toward action.

___Exhortation

d. Sensing emotional needs. Empathizing with those who are hurting and seeking to ease that pain with cheerfulness.

___Giving

e. Setting before people the Word and wisdom of God persuasively to comfort, edify or instruct.

___Leadership/Administration

f. Receiving, knowing and presenting the wisdom of God to specific situations depending upon the sensitivity of the Holy Spirit.

___Mercy

g. Researching and communicating the Word of God.

___Word of wisdom/knowledge

h. The supernatural ability to intervene as an instrument to heal through prayer and laying on of hands.

___Faith

i. A special anointing to give liberally and beyond expectation.

___Healing

j. Seeing God at work in any situation and trusting

Him to work through it with no doubt.

___Miracles
k. Organizing and leading to meet the goals of a group.

___Discerning of Spirits
l. Speaking spontaneously in a language given by the Holy Spirit unknown to the speaker.

___Tongues
m. Distinguishing genuine or spurious motives by detecting the spirit source behind a person's speech or actions.

___Interpretation of tongues
n. An event of supernatural power accompanying the servant of the Lord to authenticate a divine mission.

___Apostle
o. The ability to feed, lead and nurture the flock.

___Evangelism
p. Sensing and meeting physical needs.

___Pastor/teacher
q. Translating by the Holy Spirit the utterances of one using the gift of tongues.

(Prophecy-e, Service-p, Teaching-g, Exhortation-c, Giving-I, Leadership/Administration-k, Mercy-d, Word of Wisdom/Knowledge-f, Faith-j, Healing-h, Miracles-n, Discerning of Spirits-m, Tongues-l, Interpretation of Tongues-q, Apostle-b, Evangelism-a, Pastor/Teacher-o)

How did you do? Were you able to distinguish which gift might be yours? I first started teaching on spiritual gifts thirty years ago when we trained our summer staff for camp. It was and is my persuasion that our churches and ministries would be much more effective if we could discover people's spiritual gifts and slot individuals into positions that fit them. A prophet, who tends to be very black and white in his or her evaluation of situations, does not do well in the compassion department, so to put that person in charge of the homebound ministry would be a disaster. Some of the young people we trained were in seminary studying for the ministry, and yet had never heard of the spiritual gifts. Since then, there has been much teaching on the subject, but we find in pastoring, that many church members still don't know where they fit.

What do spiritual gifts have to do with a wise woman building her house? In our marriages and homes, we can encourage our families to take tremendous spiritual strides if we are alert to help them develop their gifts.

When our youngest daughter was in elementary school, we observed a strong gift of administration on her. She took care of her older sisters. We gave her projects to encourage her gifting. We put her in charge of aspects of family outings. She delighted in planning various activities. Today, she is the events manager for a national women's organization. She manages nation-wide conferences for thousands of women, which are held in arenas all over the country. She is operating within her gift.

Let's talk about how you distinguish your gift. This will in large part determine your calling and the kind of vessel you will be in the house. It will also free you from the guilt of taking on a responsibility when you really have no conviction to do so. You can smile sweetly and reply when asked to fill a position outside your gift, "That's really not my gift, but I'd be happy to help in…" and then name the area of your gifting.

Desire – Get to work in the church. Set up chairs; teach a class; volunteer to head up a committee; learn how to evangelize. Follow your inclinations and determine what you enjoy doing. The Holy Spirit will energize and anoint the gift within you. You will begin to lean toward the gift that "fits" you.

Development – Study the gifts. Determine which characteristics describe you and begin to try out the gift you feel you may possess. If you feel you could have the gift of evangelism, witness to your neighbors. You don't have to be a big name evangelist. If you think you might have the gift of teaching, begin by teaching children. Do you feel a call to the mission field? You might have the gift of apostle. Study about missions and go on short-term mission projects. Begin to develop the gift within you.

Delight – As you develop the spiritual gift God has given you, the peace of God will descend upon you. You will delight in serving in the area of your gifting. The opposite will prove true, as well. When you are not serving in the area of your gift, you will feel restless. You will resent having to perform the duty that has been assigned to you. You will begin to experience "burnout" and will continually feel the need for a break. But when ministering using your gift, you can't wait to get to your place of responsibility and exercise the gift God has given you. I have taught Bible classes for over forty years—ever since I was a teen-ager—and I still get a thrill from seeing the Word of God plunge deep into the spirit of one of my students. I still teach a weekly Bible study. My primary gift is teaching. I am willing to serve in other capacities, and should do so cheerfully when needed, but my drive and motivation is in the field of teaching Scripture. That is my delight.

Discernment – As you exercise your spiritual gift, others will be edified and strengthened. They will make comments like: "The Bible just opens up when you teach. I see truths I never saw before." (Gift of teaching). "I wish I could have the same kind of compassion for the poor that you have." (Gift of mercy). "You are so generous and giving." (Gift of giving). Sometimes others discern our gifts even before we do.

- In what stage do you find yourself regarding spiritual gifts—Desire, Development, Delight or Discernment?

  Or do you already know what your spiritual gift is?

- *Building Tool* – Begin to pray about your spiritual gift if you do not already know what it is. Are you serving in a capacity in which your gift can be used? Do you see the giftings that God has given your children? Are you encouraging them to use their gifts? Be prepared to discuss these areas with your group at the next meeting.

My husband and I find as we watch individuals serve in the local church and minister according to their gifts, that sometimes those differing gifts present difficulties in the marriage. This was the case for many years with my husband and myself. And we honestly did not understand what the problem was for a long time. My husband's gift is that of exhortation. He draws alongside people to comfort, encourage, rebuke and give insight toward action. He holds the office of pastor, motivated by his primary gift of exhortation.

As I stated above, my primary gift is teaching, so what was the problem? One of my secondary gifts is administration. That was the problem. One who has the gift of administration organizes and leads. That person can size up a situation, usually very quickly, and dives in to get things organized and running. For many years, my husband felt threatened by that gift. He felt that I was not being submissive to him when I began to take control of a situation.

One year we were invited to speak at a banquet in a neighboring state. Our hosts took us late in the afternoon to the church where the banquet was to be held to see the facility and the setup. There was no setup. The decorations were lying around on tables needing to be hung. The committee was standing in a corner chatting. The situation made me very nervous. Here we were—due to be back in a couple of hours to speak, and the banquet hall had not been set up.

Now, my husband's take on a circumstance like this is: "It's not my job. Don't worry about it."

My take is, "Let's get this done. You hang the crepe paper. You get the staple gun and put up the banners. You, over there, start setting up chairs. And where is the microphone—I'll set up the sound system."

I will admit my husband's approach is more gracious than mine, but when an administrator is eyeing a situation like this, graciousness is not our primary motivation. Our primary motivation is to get the job done—and get it done now. (I *have* matured a bit in this area.) I did not start giving orders, but I did climb up on a table and start hanging crepe paper. My husband was appalled. The banquet got underway—almost on time. And it was a success, as I recall.

My husband continued to be intimidated by this vast gulf of difference in our giftings and personalities until several years ago when he realized that I was simply reacting to the gift that God had deposited within me. Since then he has relaxed somewhat and enjoys watching our responses fit together like a hand in a glove to be used for God's glory. I have recently been put on staff at our church as Administrative Pastor. (For an excellent treatment on marriage and the personality differences, I suggest looking at Marita Littauer and Chuck Noon's book, *Love Extravagantly*, Bethany House Publishing, 2001).

- *Building Tool* – Discuss with your spouse the differences in your giftings. Have they been a problem in your relationship? How have you adapted to them? Perhaps you haven't searched out your spiritual gifts together—do it as a part of this assignment. Does that explain some of the tension that might have occurred in your marriage?

Accept the fact that God made you unique and gave you differing gifts in order to serve him more effectively. If you are divorced, do you feel the differences in giftings played a part in not understanding your former mate—or his not understanding you? Be prepared to discuss with your group.

In 2 Timothy 2:20-21 we find another passage pertaining to vessels in the house. As I studied all the Scriptures dealing with vessels and pottery and the Potter, this one seems to take on a different tone. I had been taught that it had the same general meaning as the other passages we just studied above. When I began to look up the meanings of the Greek words, however, the Lord showed me another perspective.

When we consider verses 14-26 in the context of the whole section, I believe we are talking not simply about vessels of honor as compared to mere common vessels, but actually vessels of dishonor—vessels that have become tainted by false teaching or godless living and which need to be cleansed before they can be used for God's glory. The Greek word for "dishonor" is *atimia,* meaning disgrace, shame, vile. Then I looked at the word in the Romans 9:21 passage—it also was *atimia.*

Commentaries give these two passages both interpretations—that of being "vessels of honor" and "vessels of common use" or "vessels of honor" and "vessels of dishonor." It seems to me in light of the meaning of *atimia*, that the meaning is much stronger than "common" and would lend itself more to the "disgrace, shame or vile" interpretation.

- Reread the Romans 9:21 passage including verses 20 and 22-24. Did God ever use the ungodly or pagans to achieve His purposes?

136

- Back up and read Romans 9:17. Whom did God use to achieve His purpose here?

  Was he a vessel of honor or dishonor?

- Read Jeremiah 27:6. Who was called a servant of God in this verse?

  Was he a believer or a pagan?

  Was he a vessel of honor or dishonor?

- Was Judas Iscariot used in the purposes of God?

  Was he a vessel of honor or dishonor?

The point is Scripture tells us that God can use anybody, believer or nonbeliever, to achieve His purposes. So it is not a question of whether or not we will be used by God. God uses all of us in His master plan. The question is: "Are we going to be used for noble purposes or ignoble, or honorable or dishonorable purposes? Are we going to be a blessing or an insult?"

According to the Timothy passage, we have a choice. The analogy breaks down a bit here, because silver goblets, pots and pans, and garbage cans have no choice as to how they will be used, but we do. Paul tells Timothy in verse 21, "If a man cleanses himself from the latter (the ignoble), he will be an instrument for noble purposes, made holy, useful to the Master and prepared to do any good work."

- Read 2 Timothy 2:14-26 to get the full context of the passage. Having read that, from what is Paul telling Timothy to cleanse himself?

- How is he to do that? (See verses 22-26.)

We do not have the power to cleanse ourselves, but we can avail ourselves of the grace and forgiveness that Jesus offers us.

- 1 John 1:9 has been called the Christian's "bar of soap." What does God promise us in this verse if we come to Him for cleansing?

Is it a partial cleansing or a full cleansing? (See the last part of the verse.)

What is our part in the cleansing?

We must apply the cleansing. We have to pick up the "bar of soap," work up the lather and spread it on our rebellious hearts, but Jesus does the work of forgiveness.

When my sister-in-law and her husband had their first baby, he was making an attempt to be helpful as she recovered from childbirth and was busy with the new baby. He decided he would mop the kitchen floor. In the middle of his chore, my sister-in-law called out to him, "Honey, what are you doing?"

"I'm mopping the kitchen floor."

"Wonderful! The soap to scrub the floor is under the sink."

"Soap?"

His intentions were good, but he was not making the right application. We can have good intentions—going to church, attending a Bible study—but if we do not make application of the Biblical truths we learn, it does us no good. If we don't "lather up" with the cleansing soap of God's Word, we are simply mopping with dirty water.

I heard a speaker several years ago who said he determined early in his walk with the Lord to always say "Yes" to God. He made a choice to keep himself cleansed and to be used as a vessel of honor for God's purposes. What an adventure we would enjoy if we would only be ready to say "Yes" to God, every time and in every situation. No need to struggle with a decision. Just say "Yes" to God—whatever God asks us to do, wherever and whenever the occasion. Simple!

- *Building Tool* – Are you willing to cleanse yourself today and say "Yes" to God whenever, wherever and whatever he asks you to do? The choice is yours. Try it for a day, a week—say "Yes" to God every time and in every situation. Speak a word of witness to that clerk in the store. Determine never to pass a homeless person without asking the Lord what he would have you do. I made that declaration after passing a homeless person by in downtown Denver one year. I was there on staff of a Christian ministry, and I passed a homeless person by without speaking a word for the Lord or giving even fifty cents! I vowed to the Lord that I would never do that again. God's Spirit pierced my heart. I backtracked to where that little woman had been, and she was gone. I was devastated. From now on, I pledged I would always say "Yes" to the whisperings of the Holy Spirit within me. Be prepared to discuss your commitment with your group and what happened as you said "Yes" to the Lord this week.

The other side of the coin is that we must determine to say "No." The Christian's sword is double-edged—we say "Yes" to the Lord, and we say "No" to the solicitations of the enemy.

As we are building our homes, a cacophony of voices shouts at us to compromise. We must say "No" to continually stand up for our "rights." Instead we are to deny ourselves, take up our crosses daily and follow Him (Luke 9:23).

We are to say "No" to watch television shows and movies that are unedifying and tempt us to ungodly living. Instead we are to think on those things that are pure, lovely and admirable (Philippians 4:8).

We are to say "No" to pursuing a career and wealth at all costs, but instead to pursue the Kingdom first (Matthew 6:33). We are to say "No" to premarital sex and extramarital sex and avoid sexual immorality and learn to control our own bodies in a way that is holy and honorable (1 Thessalonians 4:3-4). If we want to be a vessel of honor in the house, we must learn to say "No" to worldly philosophies and practices.

- Paraphrase in contemporary terms, the items Paul told Timothy he must say no to in 2 Timothy 2:14-26.

- What are some things to which you need to say "no?"

The last phrase with which we are going to deal in this lesson is "…prepared to do any good work." When we cleanse ourselves, and he sets us apart and makes us useful to his purposes, we are available to be used in many different ways. God uses all our past experiences to make us functional in the Kingdom.

Many denominations came to the camp/conference center we directed. We learned from that tenure at the center that God has his people in all the different churches and denominations, and we learned each denomination's particular bent and preferences. We gained some experience in dealing with the "tourist mindset." When God called us to Red River, NM, to run a lodge in a tourist town, we knew we could do that. We knew about tourists. We had run a camp and conference center. When God called us to pastor a non-denominational church, we knew God had prepared us through the ministry at the conference center in dealing with all denominations.

Life becomes exciting, as we trust the Lord to mold us into the vessels of honor to occupy the house. He doesn't waste anything in our lives. Surprises await us around every corner as we see how he wants to use us next. We say "Yes" to him, and "No" to those philosophies, practices and perspectives of life that are wrong and ungodly. We are vessels of honor to be put on display in the house, useful to the Master and prepared to do any good work.

- ***Small Group Discussion***: (1) Are you aware of which spiritual gift God has given you? If not, ask your group to help you discern your gift. (2) Are you serving in a capacity that uses your gift? (3) What about the spiritual gifts exhibited in your spouse and children? Discuss with your group what you think you detect in the members of your family and ask them to pray with you that those gifts might be made manifest to be used for God's glory. (4) Have the differences in your giftings caused any tension between your and your mate? Discuss. (5) Did you commit to say "Yes" to God—every time, in every situation? Tell your group your experiences resulting from that. (6) Did the Lord reveal to you philosophies, practices or perspectives that need to be cleansed from your heart? Ask your group to pray with you regarding those items. (7) Are you "ready for every good work?" Discuss with your group if you have any fear in following the Lord wholly and what he may have in store for you and your family.

The Wise Woman Builds

Chapter Eleven

Come In This House!

"Practice hospitality" (Romans 12:13).

"Come in this house!"

"Come on in!"

"Welcome!"

"Yall come!" (in the South).

 "Mi casa es su casa!" (in our part of the country—the Southwest).

However one expresses it, hospitality is a valued Christian trait. Some commentators list hospitality as one of the spiritual gifts. We did not consider it in our discussion on the spiritual gifts in the last chapter, because it is not listed in the majority of the studies on the subject;

nevertheless, it is certainly a worthy quality to be developed.

The practice of hospitality was non-existent in my family of origin. I do not remember my parents having friends over to dinner—ever—not even one time. I invited friends occasionally to spend the night when I was in elementary and junior high school, but as I became an older teen, I became embarrassed over my dad's drinking problem and ceased even that. To this day my mom has never invited us to her home for the holidays or for dinner. After we married, I assumed the responsibility of being hostess for the family.

Becoming a part of my husband's family was culture shock. I was ushered into a world of country-club activities, socials, church dinners, parties and gatherings. I had never been around anything like it. My mother-in-law was the epitome of a gracious hostess. She entertained frequently using beautiful china, silver and crystal. For each holiday she lavishly decorated every room and corner of the house. We barely managed to put up a Charlie Brown Christmas tree at our house. The first Christmas I spent with my fiancée's family, I was greeted by a sparkling tree that towered to the ceiling of their living room—gifts piled abundantly under the tree, stretching so far into the living room, one could hardly walk through. I watched my mother-in-law as she lovingly greeted people coming into their home. Each guest received a hug and a warm greeting. No one ever felt like a stranger in my husband's home. I earnestly desired our new home to reflect that Christian graciousness as well. However, entertaining was a new adventure for me— a rather daunting one at that—and I had much to learn.

Shortly after we married, my husband received a direct commission out of college as an Army 2nd Lieutenant in the Medical Service Corps. I had not a clue of what was ahead of me as an officer's wife. Even more intimidating, he became the CO (commanding officer) of an ambulance unit—that meant I was the commanding officer's wife, with many social responsibilities for which I had no training. I am sad to say that I flunked that stage of my life. I didn't enjoy the military social life. Catering to tipsy majors at a dinner/dance once a month was not my idea of fun. Being told I had to hold a drink in my hand to appear sociable, even though I had a conviction against drinking, offended my tender conscience in that area. I constantly kicked against the pricks.

Many years have passed since we were in the military, and we have matured. I realize now that instead of fighting against the system, I could have been more creative in dealing with the dilemma. I could have invited the officers and wives to our house more often. We did entertain at our home some, but not nearly enough. I could have planned outings during the day for the wives to go shopping together, or for a picnic with our children. God brought these couples into our sphere of influence, and we could have been a much more effective voice for the Lord if I had been aware of how hospitality could open the door to people's hearts.

- Turn to Genesis 18:1-8. Go through this passage and list the evidences of hospitality Abraham exhibited to the three visitors here.

- How would Abraham's actions translate into contemporary behavior?

Israel was noted for its hospitality. Not only did the Scriptures teach it, but the rabbis enjoined it in the strongest of terms. No man in Jerusalem was to consider his house his own during the feasts of Israel. All were said to be able to find gracious reception. The custom was to hang a curtain in front of the door of the home, to indicate that there was still room for guests. Some suggested that there should be four doors in every home, to bid welcome to travelers from all directions. To go out to greet a guest and then accompany him when he left was common custom. The greatest privilege was to entertain one in the rabbinical order and to send him away with gifts. One doing so received high commendation.[1]

- Turn to 2 Kings 4:8-10 and read of an example of hospitality extended to a rabbi.

- Have you made it a point to be hospitable to those who serve you in the church? Especially the pastors?

  Why or why not?

- Was the woman in the Kings passage a wise woman?

  Give reasons for your answer.

I started this book by talking about our experience of building our first house and the importance of employing a good architect and pouring a solid foundation. The second house we built was on the grounds of the conference center we directed. Because many individuals in ministry came to our center to speak, we wanted to have a nice room available for them in our

---

1   Alfred Edersheim, *Sketches of Jewish Social Life,* (Peabody, MA: Hendrickson Publishers, 1994), 47.

home. We included a special large guest room with a full, private bath and a separate outside entrance, so they could come and go without having to traffic through the main part of the house where our family was quartered. It was also accessible to the kitchen if they desired. I pray this attempt to accommodate those who ministered at our camp was a blessing to them. It was a blessing for us to provide it for them.

- *Building Tool* – If you have never invited your pastor and family to your home for dinner, would you be willing to do so? Discuss doing so with your spouse and pray about the possibility.

Being reserved, a perfectionist, and a rather private person, it has been difficult for me at times to be flexible enough to open our home for entertaining. Everything has to be perfect, don't you know? The house must be sparkling, spic and span, and the perfect table set before I can ask people into our home. Or that was how I felt. I have come to learn that is not necessarily so. What God asks is that we be willing to extend hospitality to others, not that we have a perfect house or extravagant table settings. He looks on the heart.

- Look up Luke 10:38-42 and read. Do you picture yourself as a Martha or a Mary? Give reasons for your choice.

The NIV Study Bible says that Martha and Mary were well known in the area for their hospitality and their love for Jesus and the disciples. Evidently Martha was the kind of hostess who was consumed by the voluminous details that crowd one's mind as a special dinner is being planned. I can empathize with Martha. To have someone as extraordinary, as unique, as awesome, as the Son of God come to dinner at your home must have been overwhelming. I think most of us, had we been in Martha's place, would have been obsessed, as well, with wanting to please Jesus with our cooking and our home.

However, that was not the quality Jesus commended. Jesus complimented Mary for her interest in learning about the Kingdom from Him. We lose some of the impact of Mary's courage in the text because of our western mindset. In Middle Eastern culture, the women did not eat with the men, and they certainly did not sit in on the men's conversations after dinner. Neither were women permitted to be educated. Sitting at the feet of a rabbi while he was teaching designated that person as a disciple—one who was receiving instruction. Do you see the significance of Mary's willingness to defy convention?

I gather from this passage that being hospitable involves more than a having a sparkling-clean house and serving a delicious a five-course dinner. Being hospitable is more than entertaining. Being hospitable means open arms and open hearts for one's guest—being vitally interested in the lives of one's guests. Leaving dirty dishes in the sink or on the counter until after your guests depart won't alert the local kitchen police to issue you a ticket for neglect of duty. Being hospitable is a matter of the heart. It is focusing on relationships. It is the love of Jesus overflowing out of our hearts into the lives of our guests.

- *Building Tool* - Invite guests to your home—and then relax and enjoy them. Be a Mary instead of a Martha. Don't put it off. Pick a date and set it up. Report to your group the date you selected and who is coming to dinner. We are hosting our Life Group tonight. I pledge along with you to be a Mary, not a Martha!

Jesus must have enjoyed being in the home of Mary and Martha, and their brother Lazarus. He visited frequently. They were friends. I can imagine that due to his hectic schedule and the clamoring of the people after him, sometimes he just needed a safe place to land. They must have ministered to him in many hospitable little ways that made him feel comfortable and accepted.

I have noticed that it is in the small courtesies many times that hospitality is exhibited.

- Go to Acts 21:5-6. What Jewish custom of hospitality do you see here?

- Do you practice this gracious quality in some way?
  How?

This was one of the small courtesies that I have observed as I watch Christian couples relate to their friends. Just the simple act of accompanying one's guests to the door, standing on the porch as they departed, or even walking to the car with the guests—such a modest gesture, but one of graciousness. Remaining in the recliner, glancing between one's guests and the television and waving good-bye, is a slovenly way to acknowledge visitors' departure. That it is even mentioned in Scripture is interesting, I think.

As my husband and I grew in the Lord, we began a practice of praying with couples before they left our home—speaking a blessing over guests upon their departure or praying for a concern on their hearts. Of course, we don't do that upon every occasion, but we are open to the Holy Spirit's nudges when it is appropriate to do so.

Progressing through the study, we are discovering that hospitality is mentioned frequently, directly and indirectly, in the Scriptures. One of the unexpected places we find hospitality included is in the New Testament slate of qualifications for elders.

- Turn to 1 Timothy 3:2-7 and Titus 1:6-9. List the qualifications for elders found in these two passages.

Looking at the qualifications for New Testament leadership is thought provoking, and each attribute is commendable, but what we are interested in for our study here is the quality of hospitality. Both of these lists include this gentle characteristic.

Philoxenos is the Greek word of hospitality, meaning "fond of guests." This gave me a moment of pause, because, as mentioned before, I am rather reserved by temperament and enjoy my privacy. As I was studying for this, I asked my husband, "Do you know what the Greek word for 'hospitality' means?"

"What?"

"It means 'fond of guests'."

"Oh, yeah, I remember that now. When I looked that up one time, it made me stop and think." He grinned at me knowingly.

You see, my husband is always ready for a party—if it is not too much trouble. However, being a pastor and on call basically twenty-four hours a day, he enjoys his privacy also when he can manage some.

When we come home on Sundays after worship service, both of us are ready to relax. We go in at 7 o'clock on Sunday mornings for prayer, then I go to praise team rehearsal, then teach the adult Bible class, and play the keyboard for the service. My husband preaches the sermon, and then both of us are available to pray for and minister to the needs of people. Our church does not have Sunday evening services, so we treasure Sunday afternoons to rest. In order to take a full day off, we have to travel somewhere to get away from the phone and drop-ins. We all need those get-away times. They are important for spiritual and physical refreshing. But to make withdrawal a lifestyle is not Biblical. The Christian lifestyle is one of actively penetrating our sphere of influence with the gospel.

- Look up Acts 2:42-47. List the "hospitality" attributes you find in these verses concerning the early church.

I cannot tell you how many times through the years I have taught on this Scripture. My degree is in Church Careers, and I have developed a Bible study entitled "Church Is Not A Spectator Sport," using this as the main text.

I have taught it in conferences, to our church, and in Bible studies—to youth and adults, men and women. However, I had never noticed before now how much it deals with hospitality. It is referred to indirectly, but it is hospitality, nonetheless. It is about living with open arms in community.

We Americans value our independence and privacy. The latest Barna report states that 95% of Americans consider themselves independent thinkers. We don't really know what it means to live in community. For years, our church has tried to launch Life Groups (or small groups, cell groups, family groups—whatever terminology you are familiar with). We have struggled for many reasons, but in my opinion, one of the main reasons is because we have difficulty opening our homes and being hospitable. We had rather sit in a pew and listen politely to a sermon, then go home, untouched, unmoved and unchallenged, than open our homes and be vulnerable and accountable to one another. Some of our people did not want their homes being messed up by the children in the groups. Some of the couples did not want to or did not know how to prepare dishes for a potluck dinner. These are aspects of being gracious and hospitable.

- Do you struggle with any of the aspects of hospitality mentioned in the Acts passage or maybe some of the attitudes I cited in our endeavors in our fellowship to open our homes? Name them.

- *Building Tool* – Be prepared to discuss with your group whether you agree that our independent American lifestyle has robbed the church of the power it possessed in the formative years of its development. Relate it to hospitality and give reasons for your opinion.

- 1 Peter 4:9 again tells us to be hospitable. Read the verse, then paraphrase in your own words.

In a strange sort of way, I find comfort that some in the early church were struggling to offer hospitality to one another without grumbling. I can relate to that. Nevertheless, it is a service we should give cheerfully and with pleasure. A wise woman realizes that hospitality is a privilege and not a burden.

Because I travel and speak at conferences and retreats, many times I am invited to stay in homes. I think of the times a hostess has so graciously attended to my needs—prepared food she knew I preferred, arranged beautiful flowers for me to enjoy, given me a quiet place to study and pray, placed a lovely gift basket with thoughtful items in it that I might need during the weekend. I would hate to think that ministry of hospitality was done begrudgingly and with "grumbling."

Being very task oriented, I admit I sometimes resent interruptions. However, I have come to recognize that interruptions to my schedule are sometimes God-ordained appointments. That drop-in visitor may be masking some hurt she needs to pray about. That phone call from the girlfriend who is long-winded may have a need to simply be heard. Hospitality, I am learning, is not necessarily an event. It is acceptance and love for one another. It is an "open" face to one another—a face that says "I am glad to see you!"

- Have you been guilty of grumbling when you were called upon to extend hospitality? I have. Confess it now to the Lord and ask him to give you a whole new attitude toward the privilege of opening your home for hospitality.

What about hospitality to strangers? Not only should we extend hospitality to the household of faith, but also to those who need the Lord. Our hearts and homes are to be open to strangers as well as our friends and brothers and sisters in the Lord. Scripture has something to say about that. Keep in mind Abraham's experience with the three strangers as you read this next passage.

- Read Hebrews 13:2. Why do you suppose the Holy Spirit included an exhortation to entertain strangers in this verse?

  Do you think we could *literally* entertain angels without knowing it?
  Why or why not?

- Turn to Judges 6:12-22 and 13:15-16. Has your opinion about entertaining "angels unaware" changed at all upon reading this passage?

Gideon and Manoah did not know that they were entertaining an angel in these passages. The angels' identities were revealed after the two men had offered their hospitality.

These passages remind us that we are to be hospitable to strangers, as well as those we know and love. Much of the time—no, I would be prepared to say, most of the time-- "strangers," who do not have a relationship with the Lord, will not come into a church service cold turkey. But they will come into our homes for dinner, or a couple's life group. They won't feel threatened, or overwhelmed, or intimidated in our homes like they would in a church service.

Karen Mains says in her book, *Open Heart—Open Home,*

If Christians, corporately, would begin to practice hospitality, we could play significant roles in redeeming our society. There is no better place to be about the redemption of society than in the Christian servant's home;... a Christian home is a miracle to be shared.

Another aspect to opening our homes is the fact that our homes can be role models for those around us who are struggling. Christian marriages can be examples of godly, loving, caring relationships when Jesus rules the household. Secure, happy children who lovingly obey their parents because they trust them can be a beacon of light to their friends and schoolmates who live in a home that is not a safe haven.

I shall be forever grateful to Christian friends who opened their homes to me when I was growing up. It was from their parents and siblings that I first heard genuine, carefree laughter in the home, fun at the dinner table, open discussions late at night with understanding, interested parents.

Hospitality is the door. Hospitality is the bridge. Opening our homes is a way we can build bridges to share the gospel with those who don't know Jesus in our community.

- Reread verse 47 of Acts 2. What was the result of the hospitality in this community in the early church?

Barbara Ball writes in her book, *The Joy of Hospitality, Fun Ideas for Evangelistic*

Entertaining, which she co-authored with Vonette Bright, about building bridges of friendship and relationship that will span the gap between us and our neighbors whom we would like to reach for the Lord. She says that in this modern, technological age, we know little about being good neighbors. She then makes five suggestions:

(1) Be open to your neighbors. Simply waving and saying "hi" goes a long way toward opening the door. My husband and I try to walk every day, and we make an effort to stop and chat with our neighbors as we progress along the road.

(2) Make a point of meeting your neighbors. Take homemade goodies to them or offer to pick up something at the store. When we hired the new administrative assistant at our church, she commented, "Oh, I remember when you and pastor brought cookies to the house when we moved into the neighborhood several years ago." I had forgotten about the incident, but she hadn't. In those years she had joined the church, become an active part of our fellowship and is now a vital part of our ministry.

(3) Make sure your house appears inviting. Open the draperies, put a welcome mat or wreath out, fence up any intimidating dogs.

(4) Go one more step and invite your neighbors over for a casual dinner or dessert and coffee or a game night or barbecue.

(5) Plan events for sharing of your lives together—shopping excursions, movies together, offer to pick something up at the store. Just be available.

- ***Building Tool*** – Pray and ask the Lord for some ways you can start to be more hospitable to your neighbors. Discuss it with your spouse. Plan in some small way to begin to reach out to those who live around you.

- Turn to Luke 10:25-37 and read these familiar verses relating perhaps the supreme example of hospitality found in Scripture.

A lawyer, an expert in the law, steps forward out of the crowd surrounding Jesus as he taught, and asks a question—and the Scripture says, "…to test him."

Jesus tosses the lawyer's question of "What must I do to inherit eternal life?" back with another question, "You're a lawyer. What does the law say?" (My paraphrase.)

The lawyer answers with the greatest commandment, "'Love the Lord your God with all your heart and with all your soul and with all your strength and with all your mind;' and, 'Love your neighbor as yourself.'"

- The lawyer responds to Jesus by saying, "And who is my neighbor?" Do you think you might have asked a similar question?

Jesus answers by telling a story—a story that runs through the hearts of those listening like a dagger, the Parable of the Good Samaritan. This story is perhaps too familiar. We lose the poignancy through its familiarity, but we also lose something in the translating of the account from one culture to another. Let's try to put ourselves in this scene.

- What would be your reaction if you saw someone beaten, lying alongside the road?

- What if the person lying alongside the road, beaten, was not of your race? What would you do?

- What if you couldn't discern what race or color the person was? And what if you lived in a section of the country where racial tensions were high—riots, lootings, rapes—what would you do?

- Suppose you were on your way to teach a Bible study. You are late and your immediate supervisor has told you if you are late one more time, you will have to forfeit your position as the Bible study leader. Now, what do you do?

This is somewhat of the dilemma in which the priest and Levite found themselves. The priest was constrained by his priestly duties from touching a dead man, and we don't know whether the man is dead or not. If the man was dead, contact with him would defile the priest's purity. The priest collected, distributed and ate the tithes. If he became defiled, he can do none of these things, and his family suffers the consequences. The tithes could only be eaten in a state of ritual purity.

Not only that, the rabbinical teaching of the day was this: "If you do a good turn, know for whom you are doing it, and your good deeds will not go to waste. Do good to a devout man, and you will receive a reward. If not from him, certainly from the Most High. Give to a devout man, *do not go to the help of a sinner.*"[2] (Emphasis mine.)

We can determine nothing about the man. The priest is a prisoner, caught between his tradition and compassion. What is he to do?

- Like the priest, do you think we try to answer life's problems by adhering to a list of do's and don'ts? And we feel very self righteous until we encounter a wounded person on our journey—then our safe system breaks down?

Give an example.

The Levite has similar issues as the priest, but not quite as binding. He could have stopped and given aid with not as serious repercussions as the priest. But he, perhaps having seen his superior pass by, or perhaps because of fear of being robbed himself, passes by the wounded man as well.[3]

- What is your primary fear in opening up in compassion and hospitality to one who is wounded?

To the Jewish audience, the next character they expected on the scene was a Jewish

---

[2] Kenneth E. Bailey, *Poet & Peasant and Through Peasant Eyes, A Literary-Cultural Approach to the Parables in Luke,* (Grand Rapids: Eerdmans, 1983), 43.

[3] Ibid., 46-47.

layman, a natural sequence. These three classes of people officiated in the temple. Delegations of priests, Levites and a "delegation of Israel" went up to Jerusalem and returned after their specified two weeks of religious duty, so naturally all three groups would be on the road returning home.

Much to the shock of the audience, Jesus introduces a totally unexpected third character—one from the hated Samaritan race. Centuries of hatred existed between the two races and at the time of Jesus, the bitterness was at a high peak, for just a few years earlier, the Samaritans had scattered human bones in the temple court during Passover. Jesus is speaking to the audience's deepest prejudices and painfully exposes them. He not only exposes their prejudice, but makes the hated object morally superior to their own religious leaders.

The Samaritan is bound by the same Torah as the priest and Levite. He was in the same danger posed by the robbers. He, too, was probably aware of the priest and Levite ahead of him—or if he were going in the opposite direction, actually passed them. But he feels compassion for the man. He not only dresses the wounds, but puts him on his donkey, and he walks. He transports him to an inn and *pays* for his care.

The Samaritan does all this at great risk to his personal safety. The Jewish keeper of the inn is going to initially suspect the Samaritan of being the culprit. It would be comparable to a Native American in the Old West carrying a scalped cowboy into a saloon in Dodge City, Kansas, and telling the innkeeper to take care of him.[4] Would not the innkeeper in the Old West immediately suspect the Native American of doing the horrible deed?

---

[4] Ibid., 47-53.

Jesus ends the parable by saying, "Go and do likewise." In that one penetrating, permeating, piercing statement, Jesus wipes away all of our lame excuses. Go and risk being hurt and beat up in order to assist the wounded. Go and jeopardize your own schedule to rescue one in need. Go and get dirty and bloody from another's injuries. Go and gamble being misunderstood. Go and pay the medical expenses for a member of a hated race. Go and open yourselves up to the wounded lives of others—their hurts, their differences, their walls, their hang-ups. Plain and straightforward—"Go and do likewise."

- What excuses have you been offering as an excuse not to open your heart and home up to others who may be hurt and wounded?

- *Building Tool* – What are you going to do about it Jesus' statement, "Go and do likewise?"

What we are really talking about in our discussion on hospitality, is the sharing of our lives with others; sharing what Jesus has done in our hearts and in our families. Why would we want to keep that miracle selfishly to ourselves? When I think, like David, "Who am I, O Lord God, and what is my house, that You have brought me this far?" (2 Samuel 7:18), I cannot help but praise him. God did not shower the blessing of a loving, Christian home on us for us to build bigger barns and hoard the grain of a rich harvest. He blessed us so that we in turn can bless others—so that we can share the grain of a bountiful harvest with others. A wise woman opens her heart and her home to serve others in a ministry of hospitality.

- ***Small Group Discussion***: (1) Report to your group whom you invited to dinner and if you succeeded in being a Mary instead of a Martha. (2) Have you considered having your pastor into your home for dinner? (3) Discuss the question of whether our American lifestyle has robbed the church of its power, and what part hospitality might play in that. (4) Discuss ideas for reaching out to your neighbors. (5) Discuss specifically what Jesus' statement, "Go and do likewise," means to you personally. What affect will it have on your future behavior?

- ***Idea***: To bring this entire study to a conclusion, discuss having a progressive dinner for the participants and their spouses. What a blessed experience to be in one another's homes—homes that are being built by wise women. I pray God's richest, flowing blessings on you, Wise Woman.

I would be honored to hear from you and learn insights from your life and journey to becoming a Wise Woman. Visit my website at www.goldenkeyesparsons.com or email me at GPar0719@aol.com.

PERCEPTIONS OF A WISE WOMAN

PERCEPTIONS OF A WISE WOMAN

PERCEPTIONS OF A WISE WOMAN

PERCEPTIONS OF A WISE WOMAN

PERCEPTIONS OF A WISE WOMAN

PERCEPTIONS OF A WISE WOMAN

Breinigsville, PA USA
08 November 2009
227234BV00001B/23/A